1

BILLIONAIRE
BLUEPRINT

BILLIONAIRE BLUEPRINT

DISCOVER THE SECRETS OF EXTREME WEALTH

DARRIN ELFORD

DARRIN ELFORD
PREMIUM BOOKS

ISBN: 978-1-991363-27-5 (Paperback)

eISBN: 978-1-991363-28-2 (E-Book)

First edition

Acknowledgements

Writing this book has been an incredible journey, and I could not have done it alone.

First, I want to express my deepest gratitude to my family and close friends. Your unwavering support, encouragement, and belief in me have been my greatest source of strength. Thank you for always pushing me to think bigger and dream bolder.

To the mentors and successful individuals who have shared their knowledge and wisdom with me—thank you. Your insights and experiences have shaped this book, and I am grateful for the lessons you have passed on.

To my readers—you are the reason this book exists. Whether you are just starting your journey to wealth or looking for new strategies to grow, I appreciate your trust in this process. I hope this book inspires you to take action and build the life you deserve.

Finally, to everyone who has ever challenged me, doubted me, or told me something was impossible—thank you. Your doubts fuelled my determination, and for that, I am forever grateful.

Here's to success, financial freedom, and making an impact.

Darrin Elford

Table of Contents

Introduction

What if I told you that building extreme wealth isn't just for a lucky few? What if there was a blueprint—a step-by-step guide—that could take you from where you are now to a life of financial freedom, success, and purpose?

This book is that blueprint.

Right now, you might feel stuck. Maybe you work long hours but never seem to get ahead. Maybe you want more money, freedom, and security but don't know where to start. Or maybe you've tried to build wealth before, but something always got in the way—bad advice, self-doubt, or simply not knowing what works.

You are not alone. Most people live pay-check to pay-check, believing that wealth is only for the lucky, the gifted, or those born into money. But that's a lie. The truth is that extreme wealth follows a set of **rules, habits, and strategies**—and anyone willing to learn and apply them can create financial success.

What You Will Learn

In this book, you will discover:

- How **billionaires think** differently about money, time, and opportunities.

- Why **trading time for money** will never make you rich—and what to do instead.

- How to create **passive income** and make money while you sleep.

- The **Billionaire Blueprint**—the seven laws that the world's wealthiest people follow.

- Why most people never build wealth—and how to avoid their mistakes.

- How to **manage and multiply** your money like the ultra-rich.

- Why purpose-driven wealth matters—and how to build wealth with meaning.

This Book is Not for Everyone

If you're looking for a get-rich-quick scheme, this book is not for you. **Building real wealth takes time, effort, and a shift in mindset.** But if you are ready to take control of your financial future, challenge your beliefs about money, and apply what billionaires already know, then you are in the right place.

Your First Step

By the time you finish this book, you won't just understand how wealth is built— you'll have a clear plan to create it for yourself. **Your journey to financial success starts now.**

Let's begin.

The Poverty Mindset Trap – Why You're Stuck

The Hidden Programming That Keeps You Broke

Most people don't realize they've been programmed to stay broke. From the moment you were born, society, school, and even your own family have shaped how you think about money. And if you're like most people, you were taught to survive—not to thrive.

Think about the phrases you heard growing up:

- "Money doesn't grow on trees."

- "Rich people are greedy."

- "You have to work hard for every penny."

- "It takes money to make money."

These sayings get repeated so often that they become truth in your mind. They sink deep into your subconscious, forming beliefs that control your financial decisions without you even realizing it. This is the hidden programming that keeps you struggling.

When you believe money is scarce, you act out of fear. You hesitate to take risks, you settle for low-paying jobs, and you sabotage opportunities without knowing why. When you see wealth as something only the lucky or dishonest achieve, you never seriously chase it. And when you think financial success is only for people with special talents, you convince yourself you're not one of them.

But here's the truth: None of these beliefs are real. They are illusions passed down through generations. And until you break free from them, you will stay exactly where you are—stuck.

The rich don't think like this. They don't fear money; they respect and control it. They see opportunities where others see obstacles. They don't play defense with their finances; they play offense. They understand that wealth starts in the mind, long before it appears in the bank account.

If you want to escape the poverty mindset, you must rewire your thinking. Start questioning every limiting belief you have about money. Challenge the idea that success is out of reach. Train yourself to see money as a tool, not a threat. The moment you shift your mindset, you will start to see wealth in places you never noticed before.

Because the truth is, the only thing keeping you broke isn't your job, your background, or the economy—it's the way you think. Change that, and you change everything.

A Story of Two Friends

I once knew two childhood friends—Mark and James. They grew up in the same low-income neighborhood, attended the same schools, and faced the same struggles. But their beliefs about money couldn't have been more different.

Mark always heard his parents say, "Life is hard, and rich people don't care about us." He grew up believing that making big money required luck, connections, or doing something unethical. So he never tried. He stuck with a job that paid just enough to get by and avoided anything that felt too ambitious. Deep down, he believed wealth wasn't for people like him.

James, on the other hand, had a different mindset. Even though his family was poor, his uncle once told him, "Money is just a game—if you learn the rules, you can win." That one idea stuck with him. Instead of seeing wealth as something out of reach, he saw it as something he could figure out. He read books, took risks, and surrounded himself with people who thought bigger. Fast forward ten years—Mark is still struggling, while James runs multiple businesses and is financially free.

They started from the same place. The only difference was mindset.

Your Mindset is the Lock—And the Key

When you believe money is scarce, you act out of fear. You hesitate to take risks, you settle for low-paying jobs, and you sabotage opportunities without knowing why. When you see wealth as something only the lucky or dishonest achieve, you never seriously chase it. And when you think financial success is only for people with special talents, you convince yourself you're not one of them.

But here's the truth: None of these beliefs are real. They are illusions passed down through generations. And until you break free from them, you will stay exactly where you are—stuck.

The rich don't think like this. They don't fear money; they respect and control it. They see opportunities where others see obstacles. They don't play defense with their finances; they play offense. They understand that wealth starts in the mind, long before it appears in the bank account.

If you want to escape the poverty mindset, you must rewire your thinking. Start questioning every limiting belief you have about money. Challenge the idea that success is out of reach. Train yourself to see money as a tool, not a threat. The moment you shift your mindset, you will start to see wealth in places you never noticed before.

Because the truth is, the only thing keeping you broke isn't your job, your background, or the economy—it's the way you think. Change that, and you change everything.

How Schools and Society Condition You to Think Small

From the moment you enter school, you are taught to follow the rules, stay in line, and think inside the box. You are told what to study, what to believe, and what kind of life you should aim for. But here's the problem—this system isn't designed to make you rich. It's designed to make you obedient.

Think about it. Schools don't teach you how to build wealth, invest, or start a business. They don't teach you about financial freedom or how to think like an entrepreneur. Instead, they train you to be a good employee—someone who follows instructions, works hard for a pay-check, and never questions the system.

- You are told to **get good grades** so you can get a "good job."

- You are taught to **work hard** and trade your time for money.

- You are conditioned to **fear failure** instead of seeing it as a stepping stone to success.

- You are warned that **taking risks is dangerous**, so you stick to what feels safe.

But look at the wealthiest people in the world—do they follow these rules? No. They think differently. They take risks. They build, invest, and create value. They don't just work for money; they make money work for them.

The System Was Never Meant to Make You Rich

Society teaches you that success means getting a stable job, buying a house, and saving for retirement. But this is a slow, limiting path. It keeps you in a cycle where you work for money instead of letting money work for you.

The truth is, the system doesn't reward people for thinking big—it rewards people for staying in line. That's why the wealth gap exists. The people who break free from traditional thinking—the entrepreneurs, the investors, the innovators—are the ones who create real wealth.

Breaking Free Starts with Awareness

If you want to escape the poverty mindset, you have to start questioning everything you were taught about money and success.

- Instead of thinking, *How can I get a good job?* ask, *How can I create a source of income that works for me?*

- Instead of believing, *I need to work hard for money*, shift to, *I need to make money work hard for me.*

- Instead of fearing failure, start seeing it as part of the learning process.

The world's wealthiest people weren't born with different brains. They were just exposed to different ideas. And now, so are you. The question is—will you keep thinking small, or will you start thinking like the wealthy?

Because the moment you break free from the mindset society gave you, you open the door to the life you were meant to live.

Rewiring Your Financial Beliefs and Mental Scripts

If you've been stuck in the poverty mindset, it's not your fault—but it is your responsibility to break free. The beliefs you hold about money, wealth, and success weren't chosen by you. They were handed down from your family, schools, and society. And if those beliefs are keeping you broke, it's time to rewrite them.

Think of your mind like a computer. If you're running an outdated operating system full of money-limiting beliefs, no matter how hard you work, you'll stay stuck. The good news? You can upgrade your system. You can rewrite your financial mental scripts and start thinking like the wealthy.

Identify the Lies You've Been Told About Money

Your beliefs shape your reality. If you believe money is scarce, you'll struggle to find it. If you believe rich people are greedy, you'll subconsciously push wealth away. If you believe success is about luck, you won't take control of your future.

Here are some of the most common money lies that keep people broke:

- **"Money is the root of all evil."**

  Truth: Money is just a tool. It amplifies who you are. If you're kind, money helps you do more good. If you're selfish, it magnifies that too. But money itself is neutral—it's how you use it that matters.

- **"Rich people are lucky or dishonest."**

  Truth: The majority of wealthy people built their success through smart decisions, hard work, and persistence. If you believe wealth only comes from luck or corruption, you'll never pursue it the right way.

- **"You have to work hard to make money."**

  Truth: Hard work alone doesn't make you rich. Plenty of people work long hours and stay broke. Wealth comes from working *smart*—investing, creating value, and leveraging systems that generate income without trading all your time for money.

- **"I'm just not good with money."**

  Truth: Managing money is a skill, not a talent. If you don't know how to handle money, it's because no one taught you. But you can learn, just like you learned to read, write, or drive a car.

Replace Limiting Beliefs with Wealth-Building Truths

Once you've identified the money lies holding you back, it's time to replace them with new, empowering beliefs. Here's how:

1. **Write down the old belief** – Example: "Making money is hard."

2. **Challenge it** – Ask yourself, "Is this always true? Are there people who make money easily?"

3. **Replace it with a new belief** – Example: "Money flows to me when I create value and use smart strategies."

4. **Reinforce it daily** – Read your new beliefs every morning. The more you repeat them, the more your brain will accept them as truth.

Here are some powerful financial beliefs to adopt:

- "Money is abundant, and I can create it."

- "Wealth is a result of smart decisions, not luck."

- "I am in control of my financial future."

- "Opportunities to grow my income are everywhere."

Take Action to Rewire Your Mindset

Beliefs alone won't change your life—you need action. Start surrounding yourself with people who think differently about money. Read books by self-made millionaires. Learn about investing, business, and wealth-building strategies. Take small steps toward financial independence every day.

Your old mental scripts might tell you that wealth is out of reach. But the truth is, it's just on the other side of your beliefs. Rewrite them, and you'll rewrite your future.

The First Step: A Billionaire Mindset Reset

If you want to escape the poverty mindset and step into wealth, the first thing you need to change isn't your job, your bank account, or your business—it's your mindset. The way you think about money, success, and opportunity will either keep you broke or make you rich. And right now, if you're feeling stuck, it's likely because you're operating with the wrong mental programming.

Think of your brain like a GPS. If you've been programmed with directions that lead to struggle and financial stress, no matter how hard you try, you'll keep ending up in the same place. To reach a new destination—wealth, freedom, abundance—you need to reset your GPS with the right coordinates. That means thinking the way billionaires think.

Step 1: Take Full Responsibility for Your Financial Future

The first billionaire mindset shift is ownership. Wealthy people don't blame the economy, their upbringing, or bad luck for their financial situation. They take full control.

If you're broke, struggling, or feeling stuck, the worst thing you can do is make excuses. Saying "I wasn't born rich" or "The system is against me" might feel true, but it doesn't help you. Billionaires don't waste energy complaining—they focus on solutions.

Ask yourself:

- What can I do today to increase my income?

- How can I learn the skills that will make me more valuable?

- What financial habits do I need to change?

The moment you take full responsibility for your financial future, you gain power. Because if your situation is in *your* hands, then *you* have the ability to change it.

Step 2: Stop Trading Time for Money

The poverty mindset teaches you to work hard for money. The billionaire mindset teaches you to make money work for you.

Most people believe the only way to earn more is to work more hours. But this keeps you trapped. There are only 24 hours in a day, and if you rely solely on working harder, your income will always be limited.

Billionaires think differently. They don't just work for money—they build *systems* that generate money for them. These systems include businesses, investments, and passive income streams.

Start asking yourself:

- How can I create income that doesn't depend on me working more hours?

- What skills can I learn to start building wealth instead of just earning a paycheck?

- How can I invest my money so it grows instead of just spending it?

Even if you're starting small, shifting your focus from "working harder" to "working smarter" is a game-changer.

Step 3: Think Big and Take Risks

Billionaires don't think in small, safe, or comfortable ways. They dream big, take bold actions, and understand that wealth comes from calculated risks—not playing it safe.

Most people stay stuck in the poverty mindset because they fear failure. They avoid taking risks because they don't want to lose what little they have. But billionaires know that playing small is the real risk.

Every major success story—from Elon Musk to Jeff Bezos—started with someone willing to take a chance. They weren't reckless, but they believed in their vision and acted on it.

To reset your mindset:

- Stop settling for small goals. Dream bigger.

- Take calculated risks instead of always playing it safe.

- Learn from failures instead of fearing them.

Step 4: Surround Yourself with Wealthy Thinkers

If you spend most of your time around people who think small, complain about money, and believe wealth is impossible, their mindset will rub off on you.

Billionaires surround themselves with other successful, driven, and ambitious people. They invest in mentors, read books by wealthy thinkers, and constantly learn from those who have achieved financial freedom.

Ask yourself:

- Who do I spend the most time with? Do they inspire or limit me?

- What books, podcasts, or mentors can I learn from?

- How can I put myself in environments that encourage wealth-building?

Your network and influences shape your mindset. Upgrade them, and your thinking will follow.

The Billionaire Reset Starts Now

The biggest difference between the rich and the poor isn't money—it's mindset. The good news? You can change your mindset today.

Start taking responsibility for your financial future. Stop trading time for money. Think bigger, take smart risks, and surround yourself with the right influences.

This is your reset moment. The question is: will you step up and think like a billionaire, or will you stay stuck? The choice is yours.

2

The Billionaire Mindset – Higher Level Thinking

How the Ultra-Wealthy View Money, Time and Opportunity

If you want to become ultra-wealthy, you need to start seeing the world the way billionaires do. They don't think about money, time, and opportunity the way the average person does. Their mindset is completely different—and that's exactly why they build extreme wealth while others stay stuck.

Let's break down the way the ultra-rich think so you can start shifting your own mindset today.

1. Money is a Tool, Not a Limitation

Most people see money as something they need to survive. They work for it, save it, and spend it cautiously because they fear running out. The ultra-wealthy, on the other hand, see money as a tool—something to be used strategically to create more wealth.

Instead of thinking, *"How can I save more money?"*, they ask:

- *"How can I multiply my money?"*

- *"Where can I invest to make my money grow?"*

- *"How can I use money to create more opportunities?"*

They understand that money flows to those who create value, take calculated risks, and put their dollars to work. They don't hoard cash—they invest it in businesses, real estate, and assets that generate more income.

If you want to think like a billionaire, stop fearing money and start learning how to make it work for you.

2. Time is Their Most Valuable Asset

The ultra-wealthy know something most people don't: *Money is infinite, but time is not.*

While the average person trades time for money—working 40+ hours a week for a pay-check—billionaires look for ways to free up their time and make money without constantly working. They delegate, automate, and invest in systems that generate wealth even when they sleep.

They ask themselves:

- *"Is this the best use of my time?"*

- *"How can I create income that doesn't depend on me?"*

- *"Who can do this task so I can focus on bigger opportunities?"*

They don't waste time on things that don't move them forward. Instead of watching TV for hours or getting stuck in distractions, they focus on learning, networking, and building wealth.

If you want to reach a billionaire mindset, start treating your time as your most precious resource. Guard it, invest it wisely, and stop spending it on things that don't bring you closer to financial freedom.

3. Opportunity is Everywhere—But Only If You See It

The average person waits for the "right moment" to take action. They think they need more experience, more money, or more permission before they can start building wealth. The ultra-wealthy don't think this way. They see opportunities everywhere and act on them.

Instead of saying, *"I don't have enough money to start,"* they ask:

- *"How can I find investors or partners?"*

- *"What creative ways can I fund this idea?"*

- *"What can I do today to take one step forward?"*

They don't wait for perfect conditions—they move fast, take smart risks, and learn as they go. They know that every problem holds an opportunity, and the key to wealth is spotting those opportunities before everyone else.

If you want to adopt a billionaire mindset, start training yourself to see potential instead of obstacles. Instead of saying, *"I can't,"* ask, *"How can I?"* This small shift can change your entire financial future.

Start Thinking Like the Ultra-Wealthy Today

If you want to reach extreme wealth, you must stop thinking like the average person and start thinking like billionaires do.

✅ **See money as a tool**—not something to fear, but something to use and multiply.

✅ **Treat your time as your most valuable asset**—delegate, automate, and focus on high-value activities.

✅ **Look for opportunity everywhere**—act fast, take smart risks, and always ask *"How can I?"*

The ultra-wealthy don't have superpowers. They just think differently. And the moment you start seeing money, time, and opportunity the way they do, your entire financial future will change.

Now, it's your turn. Are you ready to start thinking at a higher level?

Exponential Thinking & High-Stakes Decision-Making

If you want to build extreme wealth, you must stop thinking in small, linear steps. The ultra-wealthy don't just aim for gradual progress—they think exponentially. They look for ways to multiply results, scale businesses, and create massive impact in less time.

At the same time, billionaires are masters at making high-stakes decisions. They don't let fear or uncertainty slow them down. They analyze the facts, trust their instincts, and take decisive action. Let's break down how you can adopt this powerful way of thinking.

Exponential Thinking: The Key to Skyrocketing Wealth

Most people think in a straight line. They believe success happens in small, steady steps:

- Work hard → Get a raise → Save a little more → Retire comfortably.

Billionaires don't think this way. They ask: *"How can I achieve 10X, 100X, or even 1,000X growth?"* Instead of working harder, they look for ways to **scale massively**—whether that's through technology, investments, or innovative business models.

Here's how they think differently:

☑ **Leverage, not labor** – Instead of doing all the work themselves, they build teams, automate processes, and use systems that generate income without constant effort.

☑ **Scalability, not small wins** – They don't just start a business; they create models that can expand globally, serve millions, or generate passive income.

☑ **Impact, not just effort** – They focus on high-impact opportunities that can transform industries, not just small improvements.

💡 **Example:** Jeff Bezos didn't just build a bookstore—he built a platform that could sell anything to anyone, anywhere. That's exponential thinking.

If you want billionaire-level success, start asking yourself:

- *"How can I multiply my results instead of just improving them?"*

- *"What's the biggest possible version of my vision?"*

- *"How can I create systems that work for me, even when I'm not working?"*

High-Stakes Decision-Making: The Billionaire's Edge

Ultra-wealthy people don't sit around overthinking decisions. They make bold moves, take calculated risks, and adjust quickly when needed. They know that **speed and execution matter more than perfection.**

Here's how they make decisions differently:

☑ **They focus on upside, not just risk.**

Most people avoid risk because they fear failure. Billionaires think differently. They ask, *"What's the best possible outcome?"* If the upside is huge, they take the leap.

☑ **They trust data—but also instincts.**

They look at numbers, trends, and research. But when it's time to decide, they don't hesitate. They act fast and trust their gut.

☑ **They know that indecision is more dangerous than a wrong decision.** Most people get stuck overanalyzing, afraid of making mistakes. Billionaires know that waiting too long is often the biggest mistake. They make the best choice with the information they have and adjust as needed.

💡 **Example:** Elon Musk didn't wait for the "perfect time" to start Tesla or SpaceX. He made bold decisions, took massive risks, and learned along the way. That's why he's a billionaire.

If you want to think like a billionaire, ask yourself:

- *"What's the potential upside of this decision?"*

- *"Am I waiting too long instead of taking action?"*

- *"What's the worst that can happen—and is it really that bad?"*

Your Billionaire Mindset Shift Starts Now

If you want to reach extreme wealth, you need to start thinking and deciding differently.

🚀 **Think exponentially:** Don't settle for slow, linear growth. Look for ways to multiply results, scale, and create massive impact.

⚡ **Make bold decisions:** Don't fear mistakes—fear inaction. Take calculated risks, move fast, and trust yourself.

The difference between a billionaire and an average person isn't just money—it's how they think and act. Now, it's time for you to level up.

Are you ready?

The 'Asymmetry Principle' – Why the Rich Take Smart Risks

If you want to build extreme wealth, you must stop playing it safe. The ultra-wealthy understand a powerful concept called **the Asymmetry Principle**—and it's one of the biggest reasons they get richer while everyone else stays stuck.

In simple terms, this principle means **taking risks where the potential reward is far greater than the possible loss.** Billionaires don't take reckless chances—they take *asymmetric* risks, where even if they fail, the downside is limited, but if they win, the upside is massive.

Let's break this down so you can start using it in your own life.

Why Most People Avoid Risks (And Stay Broke)

Most people are **trained to fear risk.** They've been taught that failure is something to avoid at all costs. This is why they:

✗ Stick to "safe" jobs instead of starting businesses.

✗ Save money instead of investing in high-growth opportunities.

✗ Hesitate to take action because they're afraid of making mistakes.

But here's the problem: **avoiding risk is the biggest risk of all.** If you never take a chance, you stay stuck in the same place forever.

Meanwhile, the rich look at risk differently. They understand that **not all risks are equal**—some have a small downside but a huge upside. These are the risks worth taking.

How Billionaires Use the Asymmetry Principle

The ultra-wealthy don't bet everything on a single risky move. Instead, they **make smart asymmetric bets** where:

✓ **If they win, they win big.** (The upside is massive.)

✓ **If they lose, they lose small.** (The downside is limited.)

Here are some examples of how they do this:

💡 **Investing in Startups** – Venture capitalists like Peter Thiel invest in early-stage companies. Most of them fail, but *one* big winner (like Facebook) can return 100X or more.

💡 **Launching Scalable Businesses** – Instead of trading time for money, billionaires create businesses that can scale. Even if the first few fail, one big success can make up for all the losses.

💡 **Using Other People's Money** – Wealthy investors use leverage. They invest in real estate, stocks, or businesses with bank loans or investor capital. If the investment succeeds, they get rich. If it fails, their loss is minimized.

💡 **Testing Before Going All In** – Smart entrepreneurs don't blindly jump into a new business. They test ideas first, spending a little money to see if it works. If it does, they scale up. If it doesn't, they move on quickly with minimal loss.

How You Can Apply the Asymmetry Principle

You don't need millions to start using this principle. You just need to shift your mindset and start looking for **opportunities where the upside is much greater than the downside.**

Ask yourself:

☑ *"What's the best-case scenario if this works?"*

☑ *"What's the worst that could happen?"*

☑ *"Can I limit the downside while keeping the upside open?"*

Here's how you can use it today:

→ **Start a side business** – If it fails, you lose some time and a small investment. If it works, it could replace your income.

→ **Invest in high-upside opportunities** – Instead of just saving money, put a portion into stocks, real estate, or other assets that can grow significantly.

→ **Take calculated career risks** – Don't settle for a "safe" job if a higher-paying, high-growth opportunity exists.

→ **Expand your network** – Meeting the right people costs nothing but can open doors to life-changing opportunities.

Final Thought: Risk Is Your Best Friend (If You Use It Right)

The difference between the rich and everyone else isn't just how much money they start with—it's how they *think* about risk.

🚀 **The average person avoids risk and stays small.**

🚀 **The ultra-wealthy take asymmetric risks and multiply their wealth.**

Now, the choice is yours: Will you keep playing it safe? Or will you start making smart, asymmetric bets that could change your life forever?

Shifting from Consumer to Creator: The Wealth Mentality Shift

---

One of the most profound changes you can make on your journey to extreme wealth is shifting from a **consumer mindset** to a **creator mindset.** The ultra-wealthy don't just consume—they create. They build businesses, products, and ideas that generate value for others, and in turn, create massive wealth for themselves.

This shift in thinking is what separates those who stay stuck from those who rise to the top. When you're a consumer, you're focused on what you can get. When you're a creator, you're focused on what you can give—and that's where the true power lies.

The Consumer Mentality: The Trap Most People Fall Into

The consumer mentality is ingrained in us from a young age. We're taught to:

- **Work hard** so we can **buy things.**

- Save money for **vacations, new gadgets, or clothes.**

- Follow trends and chase after the next best thing, believing that happiness comes from owning more.

This mindset keeps you stuck in the cycle of consumption. Every pay-check goes toward buying something that provides temporary pleasure, but nothing that truly builds wealth. Consumers are always looking for the next product, service, or experience that promises happiness—but it's always fleeting.

The Creator Mentality: Building Wealth from the Inside Out

Creators, on the other hand, look at the world differently. They ask:

- *"What can I create that will add value to others?"*

- *"How can I solve problems or meet needs in ways that no one else is doing?"*

- *"What opportunities can I build that will continue to grow and provide value over time?"*

Instead of spending money to consume, they **invest** their time, energy, and resources into **creating something meaningful.** They build businesses, write books, create products, and develop services that generate income, grow their influence, and ultimately create wealth.

What Creators Know That Consumers Don't

The wealthy understand that consumption is a **one-way transaction**: you give your money, and you get something in return. But **creation is a two-way transaction.** Creators give value first, and in return, they receive the potential for unlimited wealth. Here's how the creator mindset works:

1. **Value First, Money Follows:**

   Creators focus on providing value. They build products, businesses, and ideas that solve problems, meet needs, or entertain. The more value they give, the more wealth they attract.

2. **They Leverage Time and Resources:**

   Creators understand that time is their most precious asset. Instead of spending their time consuming, they spend it creating, whether by building a business, investing, or developing new skills. They also use other people's time and resources to scale their ideas.

3. **They See Opportunities Everywhere:**

   While consumers are busy looking for ways to spend money, creators are looking for ways to generate value. They see problems as opportunities to create solutions. Whether it's a new product or a better way of doing things, creators find ways to turn ideas into profit.

4. **Risk as Investment:**

   Creators are comfortable taking risks, but not reckless ones. They see risk as part of the process of creating something valuable. When they invest in something—whether it's time, money, or energy—they're thinking long-term. The potential return far outweighs the short-term risk.

How to Shift from Consumer to Creator

The first step in shifting your mentality is recognizing that you have something valuable to give. Here's how you can start thinking like a creator:

- **Change Your Focus:** Instead of thinking about what you want to buy, think about what you can build. What knowledge, skills, or services can you offer that would solve problems for others?

- **Invest in Yourself:** Instead of spending money on things that only provide short-term satisfaction, invest in skills, education, and experiences that will allow you to create long-term wealth.

- **Build Assets, Not Liabilities:** Start creating assets that generate income, like real estate, stocks, or a business. Instead of buying liabilities that drain your wealth (like fancy cars or clothes), focus on building things that will grow over time.

- **Create, Don't Consume:** Set aside time each day to work on your own creations. Whether it's a new business idea, a side project, or an investment opportunity, begin building something that can generate wealth for you in the future.

- **Value Over Money:** Shift your focus from accumulating things to creating value. The more value you provide, the more money will naturally follow.

The Creator's Path to Wealth

Remember, the transition from consumer to creator isn't just about money—it's about **mindset**. Creators build not because they want to get rich—they build because they're driven to make an impact, solve problems, and leave a legacy. The wealth is simply a byproduct of their focus on **adding value**.

The ultra-wealthy know that wealth isn't about how much you consume, but how much you create. As you begin shifting your mindset from consumer to creator, you'll not only start attracting wealth—you'll also begin to experience the fulfilment and purpose that come with building something meaningful.

Now, it's your turn to step into the creator's mindset. What can you build today that will change your life and the lives of others?

3

Mastering Time Like a Billionaire

The 80/20 Rule: Doubling Down on What Truly Matters

If you want to master time like a billionaire, you must understand and apply the **80/20 Rule**—also known as the **Pareto Principle**. This simple yet powerful idea reveals that **80% of your results come from just 20% of your efforts.**

The ultra-wealthy have this principle wired into their daily lives. They know that to achieve extraordinary success, they must focus their time and energy on the few things that truly make the biggest impact. Rather than trying to do everything, they prioritize the small number of activities that lead to the biggest rewards.

What the 80/20 Rule Really Means

Here's the core of the 80/20 Rule:

- **80% of your results** come from **20% of your efforts**.

- This means that a small portion of your actions (the 20%) are responsible for the majority of your outcomes (the 80%).

In the business world, this plays out like this:

- **20% of your clients** likely generate **80% of your revenue**.

- **20% of your products or services** may account for **80% of your profits**.

- **20% of your activities** will result in **80% of your productivity**.

When you apply this principle, you stop wasting time on things that don't move the needle and double down on the few things that do.

How Billionaires Use the 80/20 Rule

The wealthiest individuals in the world don't try to manage every little detail. They **focus on the vital few**—the key areas that have the most potential to drive their wealth. Here's how they apply the 80/20 Rule:

1. **Focus on High-Impact Tasks:**

   Billionaires don't spend their time on low-value tasks like answering every email or checking social media constantly. Instead, they spend most of their time on high-value activities—like strategic decision-making, high-level networking, and developing new business ideas.

2. **Delegate and Outsource:**

   The 80/20 Rule encourages billionaires to **delegate** tasks that don't require their expertise. They know that their time is best spent on the areas where they provide the most value. Everything else gets handed off to a trusted team member or outsourced to an expert.

3. **Leverage Their Strengths:**

   Billionaires understand their unique abilities and double down on them. They spend their time doing the things they're best at, whether that's creating vision, negotiating deals, or making big-picture decisions. They let others handle the rest.

4. **Eliminate the Unimportant:**

   They are ruthless about cutting out the activities that don't contribute to their goals. Whether it's unnecessary meetings, low-impact projects, or time-wasting habits, they eliminate distractions to make room for what truly matters.

5. **Master the Power of Compound Growth:**

   Wealth is built by focusing on the few things that multiply over time. Billionaires know that their most valuable investments are those that grow exponentially—whether it's a successful business or a long-term financial investment. They identify these high-leverage opportunities and invest in them heavily.

How You Can Use the 80/20 Rule

You don't need to be a billionaire to start using this principle. Here's how you can apply it to your life:

1. **Identify Your Top 20%:**

   Take a look at your day, week, or month. What are the activities or tasks that have brought you the most success or productivity? These are your **20%**. Focus your time and energy on them and eliminate or minimize the rest.

2. **Delegate or Outsource:**

   Don't try to do everything yourself. Outsource tasks that aren't part of your core strengths. Whether it's hiring someone for administrative work or automating processes, freeing up your time for high-impact tasks is key to mastering time like a billionaire.

3. **Stop Chasing Every Opportunity:**

   Not every opportunity will lead to wealth. Be selective about where you invest your time, energy, and resources. Focus on the opportunities that have the potential to give you the highest returns and let the rest go.

4. **Focus on Your Strengths:**

   You don't need to be good at everything. Focus on what you're best at and invest the majority of your time in those areas. Whether it's sales, problem-solving, or innovation, doing what you excel at will bring you the greatest results.

5. **Use Leverage:**

   Find ways to multiply your efforts. Instead of trading your time for money, look for ways to scale your impact—whether through investments, building teams, or creating systems that work for you.

Final Thought: Time Is Your Most Valuable Asset

The biggest difference between those who stay stuck and those who achieve extreme wealth is how they use their time. Billionaires understand that time is finite. They know that to build massive wealth, they must focus on the **vital few** things that drive the greatest results.

By applying the 80/20 Rule, you can stop wasting time on unimportant tasks and start focusing on the actions that truly matter. This is the key to mastering time like a billionaire—and ultimately achieving extraordinary success.

The Billionaire Approach to Delegation and Leverage

When it comes to mastering time, the ultra-wealthy understand one simple truth: **you can't do it all yourself.** To build and maintain extraordinary wealth, billionaires don't just rely on their own efforts—they understand the power of **delegation** and **leverage**. These two principles allow them to multiply their impact, free up time, and achieve far more than most people ever could.

Delegation: The Art of Doing More by Doing Less

Billionaires don't spend their days stuck in the weeds of daily tasks. They **delegate**. Simply put, delegation is about **passing on tasks that don't require your specific expertise** or that are too time-consuming, so you can focus on the high-impact activities that truly drive results.

Here's how billionaires approach delegation:

1. **Delegate to Experts:**

    The wealthy understand their strengths and weaknesses. They delegate tasks that don't align with their skills to those who are experts in those areas. Instead of trying to handle marketing, HR, or financial planning themselves, they hand these tasks over to specialists who can perform them more efficiently.

2. **Empower Your Team:**

Delegating isn't just about giving away work—it's about **empowering others** to take ownership. Billionaires trust their teams to make decisions and take initiative, knowing that their people will bring fresh perspectives and solutions to the table. This not only relieves the billionaire of the burden of every decision but also creates a stronger, more productive team.

3. **Focus on What Only You Can Do:**

The billionaire knows where their time is best spent. They focus on strategic decisions, relationship-building, and the activities that directly drive their business forward. Everything else? Delegate it. Whether it's answering emails, scheduling meetings, or overseeing day-to-day operations, these tasks are best left to someone else.

Leverage: Doing More with Less

Leverage is the principle of using **resources, systems, and people** to achieve more with less effort. It's about making your time, money, and energy **work harder for you**. Billionaires are masters of leverage—they know that by harnessing the right resources, they can accomplish more than what's possible with their own effort alone.

Here's how billionaires use leverage to their advantage:

1. **Leverage Other People's Time:**

One of the most powerful forms of leverage is using other people's time to get things done. Billionaires build teams of talented individuals who help them execute ideas, launch projects, and scale businesses. By hiring and empowering the right people, they can focus on what truly matters, while their team handles the rest.

2. **Leverage Systems and Technology:**

Billionaires also use **systems and automation** to streamline processes and improve efficiency. Whether it's using software to manage projects, automating customer service, or employing AI for decision-making, technology allows them to handle far more with less. They set up systems that run on their own, enabling them to scale faster and smarter.

3. **Leverage Money Through Investments:**

   The wealthy don't just work for money—they make their money work for them. They understand the power of **investing**—whether it's in stocks, real estate, or businesses. With smart investments, they can generate passive income, compound wealth, and multiply their financial returns without having to trade hours for dollars.

4. **Leverage Relationships:**

   Successful billionaires know that relationships are a form of leverage. They invest time in building strong networks of people who can open doors, offer advice, or help move projects forward. Whether it's a business partner, an advisor, or a mentor, relationships are a key asset that provides leverage in both business and life.

How You Can Apply Delegation and Leverage

You don't need to be a billionaire to start using delegation and leverage. Here's how you can begin applying these principles today:

1. **Identify Tasks You Can Delegate:**

   Start by identifying the tasks that take up your time but don't directly contribute to your goals. These are the tasks you can delegate. Look at areas like admin work, customer service, or tasks that require skills you don't have but can hire someone for.

2. **Build a Reliable Team:**

   Surround yourself with people who complement your strengths and handle tasks you don't want to or can't do yourself. Trust your team to execute their areas of expertise and empower them to take ownership of their work.

3. **Leverage Technology:**

   Take advantage of technology to automate and streamline your processes. There are countless tools available today—project management software, marketing automation tools, and financial apps—that can save you hours each day.

4. **Make Smart Investments:**

Instead of spending your time working for money, focus on how you can make your money work for you. Whether it's investing in real estate, stocks, or starting a business, find ways to create streams of passive income.

5. **Network and Build Relationships:**

Use the relationships around you as leverage. Invest in meaningful relationships with people who can help you grow. Seek out mentors, business partners, and collaborators who can support your vision and provide the connections you need.

The Billionaire Mindset: Time is Your Most Valuable Resource

Ultimately, billionaires approach delegation and leverage with one simple truth in mind: **time is their most valuable resource**. They know that they can always make more money, but they can never get back wasted time. By delegating effectively and leveraging people, systems, and resources, they create a powerful, scalable operation that allows them to do more with less.

If you want to master time like a billionaire, the key is not to try and do everything yourself. Instead, **focus on what you do best**, surround yourself with the right people, and use systems and investments to work smarter, not harder. This is the billionaire approach to time—and it's how they achieve extraordinary success while working less.

How to Create More Free Time While Making More Money

One of the most powerful secrets billionaires understand is how to **create more free time while making more money**. It sounds counterintuitive, right? Most people think that the only way to increase their wealth is to work harder, longer, and sacrifice more of their personal time. But the truth is, the most successful people in the world have figured out how to **work smarter, not harder**. Here's how they do it—and how you can too.

1. Focus on High-Impact Activities

The first step to creating more free time while making more money is to focus on **high-impact activities**—the things that directly contribute to your wealth. For billionaires, this means they spend most of their time on tasks that move the needle in a significant way.

What does this look like?

- Instead of getting lost in daily, low-priority tasks, billionaires invest their time in things like **strategic decisions, building partnerships, and creating new opportunities**.

- They know that small actions often have **disproportionate results**, so they double down on activities that drive the biggest rewards. This approach allows them to **generate more wealth** while doing less.

2. Automate and Systematize

To create more free time, you have to **automate** and **systematize** as much as possible. Billionaires don't spend their time on repetitive tasks like scheduling meetings, tracking invoices, or organizing files. They set up systems that run themselves.

How can you do this?

- Start by using **automation tools** to streamline repetitive tasks—things like automating your email campaigns, using financial software to track expenses, or setting up scheduling apps to book appointments without lifting a finger.

- Create processes for everything—from your daily routine to your business operations. **Document** how things should be done and set up systems that run smoothly without your constant input. The more you set up processes that **automate your time**, the more free time you create for yourself.

3. Delegate Like a Pro

One of the most crucial secrets to freeing up time while still making money is **delegation**. Billionaires don't try to do everything themselves. They understand that **delegating tasks to experts** not only saves time but also ensures those tasks get done better and faster.

Here's how to delegate effectively:

- **Identify your strengths**: Focus only on the areas that require your specific skill set or vision. Everything else can be delegated to someone who is more qualified for the task.

- **Trust your team**: Once you've built a reliable team, empower them to handle the work. Don't micromanage—give them the tools, the freedom, and the responsibility to execute on their own.

- **Outsource**: Whether it's hiring a virtual assistant, working with a consultant, or outsourcing tasks like marketing or customer service, find ways to offload work that doesn't need your personal touch.

By delegating effectively, you not only create more free time for yourself but also **increase productivity and efficiency** within your business.

4. Invest to Multiply Your Money

Billionaires don't just work for money—they make their money **work for them**. Investing is a key way to generate **passive income** that grows over time without requiring a constant time investment.

How can you start investing?

- **Real estate**: Rental properties or real estate investments can create a steady stream of passive income.

- **Stocks**: With smart investing, you can make your money grow while you focus on other things.

- **Business**: Invest in businesses that generate returns without you needing to be involved in the day-to-day.

By putting your money into smart investments, you can start to see a **steady income** that allows you to enjoy more free time, without sacrificing financial growth.

5. Set Clear Boundaries

To create more free time, it's important to set clear boundaries around your time. Billionaires know that saying **"no"** to the wrong opportunities is just as important as saying "yes" to the right ones.

Here's how to set boundaries:

- **Limit distractions**: Eliminate time-wasters like excessive social media, meetings without purpose, or unnecessary email checking.

- **Protect your time**: Set strict office hours or block off time for personal activities. Don't let your work bleed into your personal life.

- **Prioritize high-value activities**: Focus on what brings the most reward— whether it's financial, personal, or professional. Make sure every commitment you take on aligns with your bigger goals.

By protecting your time and being intentional about where you place your energy, you can create more free time while ensuring your financial goals are still being met.

6. Use Your Time to Build Wealth, Not Just Earn It

The difference between someone who creates wealth and someone who simply earns a pay-check is in how they use their time. Billionaires don't just work for money—they build wealth through assets, investments, and business opportunities.

Shift your mindset to create wealth:

- Start thinking about **long-term opportunities** instead of short-term gains. Rather than focusing solely on earning more money through your job or business, focus on creating income streams that require little time once established.

- **Think in terms of building assets**: Whether it's intellectual property, business equity, or real estate, focus on creating things that generate income without needing constant effort.

By using your time to build wealth rather than just earn it, you can ultimately achieve more while working less.

Conclusion: Work Smarter, Not Harder

The key to creating more free time while making more money is to **be strategic** with how you use your time, energy, and resources. Billionaires don't work harder—they work smarter. They focus on high-impact activities, delegate tasks, automate systems, and make their money work for them.

You can start applying these principles today, by identifying tasks you can delegate, automating processes, setting boundaries, and investing in income-generating opportunities. With the right approach, you can **create more freedom in your life**, both financially and personally—while making more money than you ever thought possible.

The 'Money vs. Time' Equation: Stop Trading Time for Money

One of the most powerful mindsets that billionaires adopt is the realization that **money** and **time** are not the same thing. In fact, they understand that **time** is far more valuable than money. If you're still trading hours for dollars—working for a pay-check, only to repeat the process the next day—you're stuck in what I call the "Money vs. Time" trap.

The Trap of Time for Money

Most people have been conditioned to think that the only way to earn money is by working harder and longer. It's a simple equation: more hours equals more pay. This is how many jobs are structured, and for the majority of people, it's how they survive financially. But this mindset is **limited**. You can't keep working forever, and there will always be a cap on how much time you can exchange for cash.

Billionaires, on the other hand, break free from this limitation. They know that while **money** is something you can earn, **time** is a fixed resource. The reality is that you can always earn more money, but once time is gone, it's gone forever. So, the real secret to wealth isn't about how many hours you work, it's about **how you make your money work for you**.

The Wealthy Perspective: Time as the Ultimate Asset

Billionaires see **time** as their most precious asset. They understand that they can always make more money—by investing, building businesses, or creating valuable products and services—but they can never get more time. This is why they prioritize their time above all else.

Instead of trading hours for dollars, they focus on creating **income streams** that **generate money without constant time investment**. This could mean building a business that runs without their day-to-day involvement, investing in assets that grow passively, or leveraging their expertise and networks to create opportunities that work for them, rather than the other way around.

The Shift: Working for Results, Not Hours

To stop trading time for money, you must make the shift from **"working for pay-checks"** to **"working for results"**. This requires a significant mental shift. Billionaires invest their time in things that have the potential for **exponential returns**. They spend time on activities that create long-term wealth, rather than short-term rewards.

For instance, instead of spending 40 hours a week at a job, you could spend that same time **building something scalable**—a business, an investment portfolio, a product, or a brand—that generates income even when you're not working. This is **leverage** at its finest. And the beautiful part is, it's a choice you can make today.

How to Break Free from the Time-for-Money Trap

1.   **Start Thinking in Terms of Leverage**

> Leverage is the idea of using your resources—whether it's time, money, or people—to create an outcome that requires less effort on your part. For example, instead of working for someone else, you could create a business that leverages other people's time and expertise. By doing this, you're not only creating more income, but also **freeing up your own time**.

2.   **Build Passive Income Streams**

> To escape the time-for-money equation, you need to create income streams that don't require you to constantly exchange your time for cash. **Rental income, dividends from stocks, royalties from books or inventions, or automated online businesses** are all examples of passive income. Once these streams are established, they allow you to earn money without working for it day in and day out.

3.   **Outsource and Delegate**

> Billionaires know that they cannot—and should not—do everything themselves. To free up time, they hire people to handle tasks that they either don't enjoy or aren't the best at. You can do the same by **delegating tasks**, whether in your business, personal life, or day-to-day responsibilities. When you free up your time by having others do the work, you can focus on activities that have a higher return on investment.

The Key Takeaway: Time is More Valuable than Money

If you're still stuck in the trap of trading your time for money, it's time to rethink your approach. The real wealth-building secret is to **maximize your time**—to use it wisely and invest it in ways that allow you to grow wealth without constantly exchanging hours for dollars. By shifting your mindset from "working for money" to "creating wealth through leverage," you'll find that you can make more money while working less.

Billionaires don't let their time get eaten up by tasks that don't create wealth. Instead, they invest it in opportunities that will pay off for years to come. You can do the same—if you're willing to stop seeing time as just another resource to trade and start treating it as the priceless asset it truly is.

4

The Billionaire Blueprint – The 7 Laws of Extreme Wealth

The Law of Wealth Creation: Value Over Time

When it comes to building extreme wealth, there's one fundamental truth that every billionaire understands: **wealth is created through value, and that value grows exponentially over time**.

This is the foundation of the **Law of Wealth Creation**. While many people chase after quick wins and immediate gratification, billionaires think differently. They focus on creating **lasting value** that compounds over time. This is where the real wealth is built—not in a matter of weeks or months, but years and decades.

The Power of Compounding Value

One of the most powerful concepts in wealth creation is **compounding value**. In simple terms, it means that when you create something valuable—whether it's a product, service, business, or even knowledge—its value grows over time. And as it grows, it attracts more opportunities, more customers, and more capital.

Think about a successful business. At the beginning, it might require a lot of effort, time, and investment to get it off the ground. But as the business becomes more established and its value is recognized, it starts to generate **passive income**. The effort you put in today compounds, leading to greater returns in the future, often without needing to put in the same amount of work.

This is how billionaires create wealth: by building **something of enduring value** that will pay off **over time**.

Building Lasting Value, Not Quick Cash

The common mistake many aspiring entrepreneurs make is focusing on **quick profits**. They want fast results, immediate gratification, and easy wins. But quick cash doesn't build real wealth—it's just a momentary gain. True wealth comes from **building something that adds value to the world** over the long term.

Take a moment to think about the most successful companies in the world— Apple, Amazon, Tesla, Microsoft. None of these companies were built overnight. They all started with an idea, a vision, and a commitment to adding real value to people's lives. And over time, their value compounded, growing exponentially. That's why they are worth billions today.

The key lesson here is: **Focus on value creation**, not just on making money. The more value you create, the more wealth you will attract over time. When you're focused on solving real problems and offering real solutions, the wealth naturally follows.

How to Apply the Law of Wealth Creation

1. **Invest in Long-Term Projects**

   Instead of jumping from one short-term opportunity to another, focus on long-term projects that have the potential to create lasting value. Think of ways to solve big problems or meet significant needs that people will pay for—not just today, but for many years to come.

2. **Build Systems, Not Just Products**

   Billionaires don't just create one-off products; they build systems that can run and scale over time. These systems can be businesses, investment portfolios, or even personal brands. Systems have the ability to generate value continuously, long after the initial effort.

3. **Focus on Impact, Not Income**

   When you focus on the **impact** your work will have, the money will follow. The more people you help, the greater the return on your efforts. Make it your mission to create solutions that truly add value to people's lives and your wealth will grow as a natural byproduct.

The Big Picture: Value as the True Measure of Wealth

The Law of Wealth Creation is simple: **create value, and let time do its work**. While others are chasing after the next quick buck, you'll be focused on building something that stands the test of time. Your wealth will grow steadily, compounding over time, and before you know it, you'll have created a legacy that's worth far more than just money—it will be a **lasting impact** that continues to grow.

Billionaires aren't obsessed with the money in their bank accounts. They're obsessed with creating value that stands the test of time. The wealth they build is just a byproduct of the value they've created.

By following the **Law of Wealth Creation**, you can shift your focus from short-term gains to long-term success, and start building the kind of wealth that lasts for generations.

The Law of Ownership: Controlling Assets vs. Selling Time

One of the core principles that separates the ultra-wealthy from the rest is their deep understanding of **ownership**. While many people trade their time for money—working a job or offering services—the wealthiest individuals know that **true wealth comes from controlling assets**, not from selling their time. This is the **Law of Ownership**: to build extreme wealth, you must own things that grow in value over time, rather than merely exchanging your time for a paycheck.

The Trap of Selling Time

For most people, their primary source of income is their **time**—whether it's as an employee working for a salary or as a freelancer trading hours for money. This model seems logical: the more hours you work, the more money you make. But here's the flaw: **time is finite**, and you can only sell so many hours before you run out. No matter how hard you work, there's a ceiling to how much you can earn. Your time is a limited resource.

This is the trap that most people fall into—they spend their entire lives selling their time, never accumulating enough assets to break free from the cycle. It's an exhausting cycle, and no matter how many hours you put in, it's nearly impossible to achieve **true wealth**.

The Power of Owning Assets

On the other hand, billionaires understand that **ownership** is the key to long-term wealth creation. When you own assets, whether it's real estate, businesses, stocks, intellectual property, or other valuable resources, you don't have to trade time for money. **The value of your assets grows over time**, often without your direct involvement. The more assets you own, the more wealth you build.

Assets work for you. They generate passive income, appreciate in value, and create opportunities for further wealth-building. For example, owning a property may bring in rental income, while its value appreciates. Owning a company can lead to profits and equity growth, allowing you to reinvest and expand. **The real wealth-building strategy isn't about working harder; it's about working smarter—by accumulating assets that generate income with minimal time investment.**

Why Ownership is Non-Negotiable for Extreme Wealth

When you own assets, you gain control over your financial future. You're not relying on someone else to pay you for your time. Instead, you're in control of the wealth-creation process. Assets grow in value, create income streams, and generate opportunities that come with minimal effort once they're established.

Billionaires don't just work for a pay-check—they create and acquire assets that provide long-term security. The reason they build wealth is because they own things that continue to increase in value, even while they sleep. They understand that **assets can be leveraged, scaled, and passed down to future generations**, ensuring the long-term growth of their wealth.

How to Apply the Law of Ownership

1. **Start Acquiring Income-Producing Assets**

    The first step in applying the Law of Ownership is to start acquiring **assets that produce income**. This could include investing in real estate, starting a business, buying stocks, or even acquiring intellectual property. The key is to focus on assets that will create ongoing revenue, freeing you from the need to exchange your time for money.

2. **Build Systems that Generate Wealth**

    Think of ways to build **systems**—businesses, investment portfolios, or even automated online ventures—that can generate wealth without constant involvement. The more you can put these systems in place, the more you'll have ownership over your wealth, and the less you'll be tied to trading time for cash.

3. **Focus on Long-Term Value, Not Immediate Gains**

    Ownership requires patience. Rather than seeking quick returns, focus on acquiring assets that will appreciate in value over time. Whether it's buying undervalued real estate, investing in high-potential startups, or building a business with strong growth potential, it's important to think about **the long game**. Billionaires build their wealth by making decisions that benefit them over the long term, not just in the immediate future.

4. **Leverage Your Assets**

    Once you've acquired assets, don't just sit on them—**leverage** them. Use the wealth generated by one asset to acquire more. Use your growing portfolio to invest in new opportunities. The more you own, the more you can leverage your resources to create additional income streams and increase your wealth.

The Bottom Line: Own, Don't Sell

To truly break free from the cycle of trading time for money, you must shift your mindset and start **owning** rather than selling. The wealthy know that **ownership** is what builds true wealth over time. They control assets, which appreciate, generate passive income, and provide ongoing opportunities for growth. **By controlling assets, you take ownership of your financial future and unlock the path to extreme wealth.**

Remember, it's not how many hours you work—it's what you own that will create the lasting wealth you desire.

The Law of Leverage: Scaling with Systems, People & Technology

---

One of the most powerful concepts that separates billionaires from the rest of us is their ability to scale their wealth. They don't just work harder—they **leverage** their resources to do more with less. This is the **Law of Leverage**: the ability to **scale** with **systems, people, and technology** to exponentially increase your results while minimizing effort.

The Power of Leverage

At its core, leverage is about getting more out of what you have. It's about making **small inputs** result in **big outputs**. The ultra-wealthy understand that to build extreme wealth, they need to maximize their effectiveness by using **other people's time, effort, and expertise**—and the right tools to scale their vision.

Think of it this way: if you're doing everything by yourself, you're limited by the amount of time you can personally dedicate to each task. But when you leverage the right systems, hire the right people, and use the right technology, you can scale much faster and accomplish things that would have been impossible alone.

Leverage Through Systems

Billionaires understand that to scale, you need **systems** in place. A system is a repeatable, efficient process that allows you to do the same thing over and over with little to no extra effort. Whether it's an automated sales funnel for your business, a set of operational procedures for your team, or a proven method for creating value, **systems** are what allow you to scale your efforts and grow without burning out.

For example, a successful business doesn't rely on the constant input of the owner. Instead, it runs smoothly through **systems**—processes that can be replicated, improved, and scaled. These systems allow billionaires to keep operations running efficiently, increase output, and generate more revenue with less input.

Leverage Through People

The next form of leverage is **people**—specifically, the right people. Billionaires know that to scale, they can't do everything themselves. They hire top-tier talent who share their vision and can execute their ideas on a larger scale.

Leverage through people means **building a team of skilled, motivated individuals** who can carry out tasks that you would otherwise have to do. This allows you to focus on the big picture—strategizing, innovating, and creating new opportunities—while your team handles the execution.

Great leaders understand that their success isn't just about their personal skills, but about assembling and empowering a high-performing team. When you can **delegate effectively**, you multiply your productivity without multiplying your hours worked.

Leverage Through Technology

The third pillar of leverage is **technology**. In today's world, technology is one of the most powerful tools for scaling a business. It allows you to automate tasks, streamline operations, and reach a global audience with minimal effort.

Think about the way technology has transformed entire industries. **Software**, **apps**, and **online platforms** have given businesses the ability to operate at a much larger scale than ever before. From automating marketing to using artificial intelligence for customer service, technology enables you to leverage resources that would otherwise require significant human effort and time.

Billionaires use technology to create systems that allow them to run large enterprises with just a fraction of the time and resources they would need otherwise. They know that investing in technology can pay huge dividends, allowing them to scale faster and with greater efficiency.

How to Apply the Law of Leverage

1. **Build Scalable Systems**

   To leverage your efforts, start by creating systems that allow you to streamline your work. Whether it's automating your marketing, creating standard operating procedures, or designing workflows that can be repeated efficiently, systems are the backbone of scalability. Focus on creating processes that save you time and effort while delivering consistent results.

2. **Hire and Empower the Right People**

   As your business or wealth grows, you'll need help to handle the increased workload. But don't just hire anyone—hire people who are skilled, driven, and aligned with your vision. Build a team that can take on responsibilities so you can focus on higher-level strategic decisions. When you empower the right people, you free yourself from the daily grind and allow your wealth-building efforts to multiply.

3. **Invest in Technology**

   Leverage technology to automate tasks and processes that can be done more efficiently with tools and software. From customer management to accounting and marketing, there's technology available to handle nearly every aspect of your business or wealth-building strategy. **Automating** routine tasks gives you more time to focus on strategic decisions, while **scaling** your operations at a fraction of the cost and time it would take to do everything manually.

The Big Picture: Work Smarter, Not Harder

The Law of Leverage teaches us that **working smarter, not harder** is the key to building extreme wealth. By using systems, people, and technology, you can scale your efforts and multiply your results with less effort.

Billionaires don't try to do everything themselves—they leverage their time, expertise, and resources to achieve more with less. They understand that wealth isn't just about how much time you put in—it's about how effectively you use your resources.

By embracing the power of leverage, you can start scaling your own wealth-building efforts, creating opportunities that multiply over time. It's not about working harder; it's about working smarter, and using leverage to unlock exponential growth.

The Law of High-Return Investments

One of the defining characteristics of the ultra-wealthy is their ability to make money work for them. While most people focus on earning income from their job or business, billionaires think about **investing** their money in ways that create massive returns over time. This is the **Law of High-Return Investments**: the principle of strategically placing your money in opportunities that generate **significant, consistent profits** with the least amount of risk.

What Are High-Return Investments?

High-return investments are opportunities that generate a **disproportionate amount of profit** relative to the amount of money or time you put in. The key here is not simply making money—but making **smart money moves** that multiply your wealth. High-return investments often involve risk, but the rich have mastered the art of minimizing and managing that risk through careful research, diversification, and timing.

Think of it like planting a tree. You don't just plant seeds in random spots and hope they grow—you **select the right soil, nurture the roots,** and wait for them to grow strong enough to yield fruits year after year. High-return investments work in a similar way: **they may require patience, strategy, and effort upfront, but with the right approach, they produce extraordinary results over time**.

The Power of Compound Interest

One of the most powerful concepts in high-return investing is **compound interest**. This is when your investment generates not only returns on the money you initially invested, but also on the profits that have accumulated over time.

Billionaires know that the key to amassing vast wealth is to **make their money work for them**. They don't spend their profits—they **reinvest them** into opportunities that create even more wealth. This is the true magic of compound interest: as your money grows, it grows faster and faster, like a snowball rolling downhill.

For example, if you invest $100,000 with a 10% annual return, you'll have $110,000 after one year. But in the second year, that 10% will apply to $110,000— not just the original $100,000. Over time, this compounding effect can turn modest investments into significant fortunes.

Where to Find High-Return Investments

Billionaires are often looking for investment opportunities that have the potential to **explode in value**. These can range from stocks and real estate to private equity and startups. But they're not just randomly throwing money into anything that seems promising. They approach investing strategically and focus on high-return opportunities that have a **clear path to success**.

Some common high-return investments include:

- **Stocks and Equity**: When you buy shares of a company, you are investing in its potential to grow. Smart investors seek out companies with a history of innovation, profitability, and market leadership, positioning themselves to benefit as the company expands.

- **Real Estate**: Real estate is a classic high-return investment because it tends to appreciate over time, especially when purchased in high-demand areas. Real estate also provides opportunities for **rental income**, another source of ongoing returns.

- **Private Equity and Startups**: Billionaires often invest in startups or private companies, looking for opportunities that could one day become **industry leaders**. The risk is high, but the returns can be astronomical if the company grows rapidly or gets acquired for a large sum.

- **Alternative Assets**: High-return investments don't always fit into traditional categories like stocks and bonds. Billionaires also invest in things like **art, luxury goods, collectibles**, and even **cryptocurrency**—assets that can increase in value significantly.

Managing Risk in High-Return Investments

While high-return investments have the potential for great rewards, they also come with greater risks. The key to successful investing is not avoiding risk altogether, but rather **managing it effectively**.

Billionaires understand that risk is inevitable, but they make calculated decisions to mitigate it. They use tools like **diversification, hedging**, and **due diligence** to reduce their exposure to risky ventures. By spreading their investments across different asset classes and industries, they avoid putting all their eggs in one basket, ensuring that a single failure doesn't derail their wealth-building strategy.

The Power of Patience

High-return investments don't always produce immediate results. In fact, many of the best investments require **patience**. The ultra-wealthy aren't interested in making a quick buck—they're building wealth for the long term.

This long-term mindset allows them to ride out temporary market fluctuations and keep their focus on the bigger picture. They know that wealth is built **over time**, not overnight.

For example, many of the world's wealthiest individuals made their fortunes by holding onto investments for decades—letting their money compound, grow, and multiply. Rather than chasing short-term gains, they focus on making smart decisions that will pay off in the years and decades to come.

How to Apply the Law of High-Return Investments

1. **Do Your Research**

    Before making any investment, do thorough research. Understand the potential risks, rewards, and timelines involved. Billionaires don't invest in things they don't understand. They study the market, trends, and the industries they're investing in to make informed decisions.

2. **Diversify Your Portfolio**

    Diversification is one of the most powerful ways to manage risk in high-return investments. Don't put all your money into one stock, property, or asset. Instead, spread your investments across multiple opportunities to reduce your exposure to any one failure.

3. **Reinvest Your Profits**

    The rich don't spend their profits—they **reinvest them** into new high-return opportunities. By doing so, they take full advantage of the power of compound interest. Each reinvestment brings your wealth closer to exponential growth.

5. **Reinvest Your Profits**

High-return investments require patience. Don't expect to get rich overnight. Instead, think long-term and focus on building wealth over time. This mindset allows you to weather inevitable ups and downs in the market and reap the rewards of your investments in the future.

The Big Picture: Making Your Money Work for You

The Law of High-Return Investments is about creating wealth through smart decisions and strategic placement of your money. By focusing on investments that provide substantial returns over time, and managing your risks wisely, you can build a fortune that continues to grow year after year.

Billionaires know that wealth is not about working harder—it's about **making your money work for you**. By investing in high-return opportunities, you can start building your own wealth that will multiply as your investments compound over time.

The Law of Asymmetry: Finding 10X Opportunities

One of the most powerful laws of extreme wealth is the **Law of Asymmetry**— the ability to find opportunities where the potential reward far outweighs the risk. The ultra-wealthy have a knack for identifying these kinds of opportunities, where the upside is **massive** and the downside is **limited**. In other words, they look for situations where they can earn **10 times** (or more) the amount of money they invest, with very little to lose.

This principle is simple but incredibly effective. Instead of seeking small, incremental gains, billionaires go for opportunities that have the potential to **explode in value**. They are constantly on the lookout for **asymmetric bets**— situations where the **reward is disproportionate to the risk**.

What Does Asymmetry Mean in Wealth-Building?

In financial terms, **asymmetry** refers to a situation where the **possible reward** from an investment or decision is **much greater** than the potential loss. This is the opposite of traditional, low-risk investments, where the potential gains and losses are more balanced. In asymmetry, the goal is to take on a small amount of risk with the possibility of earning exponentially larger returns.

For example, if you invest $10,000 into a startup, and it grows into a billion-dollar company, you could see your initial investment multiply by 100X, 1000X, or more. On the other hand, if the startup fails, your loss is capped at your $10,000 investment. This **asymmetrical risk-reward** ratio is what billionaires seek when making financial decisions.

The Power of 10X Thinking

Billionaires don't just look for opportunities that give them a 2X or 3X return— they are searching for **10X opportunities**. These are the game-changers, the ones that have the potential to generate **ten times the return** on investment.

This is **10X thinking**: the idea that instead of aiming for small wins, you focus your energy on finding opportunities that will give you **massive rewards**. It's not about putting all your eggs in one basket, but about finding the basket that will give you **life-changing returns**.

Take the example of early investors in companies like **Amazon**, **Google**, or **Apple**. They didn't just get a small return on their money—they saw their investments skyrocket by **thousands of times**. The investors who saw the potential for these companies and took the risks were rewarded handsomely, while those who played it safe with lower-risk investments didn't see nearly the same returns.

How to Find 10X Opportunities

The key to finding 10X opportunities lies in recognizing **untapped potential**. The ultra-wealthy have the ability to identify trends, industries, or technologies that are in their infancy but have the potential to explode. Here's how they do it:

1. Think Long-Term

Billionaires don't chase short-term gains. They invest in **long-term opportunities** that have the potential to **transform industries** or even society itself. They are often early adopters, betting on ideas that others might dismiss as "too risky" or "too far out there."

By thinking long-term, you position yourself to capitalize on the **next big thing** before it becomes mainstream. You may have to wait a few years for your investment to pay off, but when it does, the returns can be **life-changing**.

2. Look for Market Inefficiencies

The best 10X opportunities often come from **market inefficiencies**—gaps or problems in the market that haven't yet been addressed. Billionaires spot these inefficiencies and **innovate** to fill the gap. This might mean developing a product or service that solves a widespread problem, or investing in a market that's **underdeveloped** but on the verge of massive growth.

For instance, the rise of **smartphones** created a huge market inefficiency. Early investors in companies like **Apple** and **Samsung** saw the potential for smartphones to become ubiquitous, and they reaped huge rewards by betting on the growth of this industry early on.

3. Embrace Technology and Innovation

Billionaires know that **technology** and **innovation** are the driving forces behind the most lucrative opportunities. By staying ahead of technological trends and investing in cutting-edge industries like **artificial intelligence, blockchain**, and **renewable energy**, they place themselves in a position to benefit from **massive advancements** that could disrupt entire industries.

For example, early investors in **Bitcoin** saw the potential of blockchain technology, and those who took a risk on it early have made extraordinary returns. Similarly, companies like **Tesla** disrupted the automotive industry by embracing electric vehicles long before they became mainstream.

4. Take Calculated Risks

The ultra-wealthy understand that risk is an inherent part of wealth-building. However, they don't gamble recklessly—they take **calculated risks**. This means doing thorough research, analyzing the potential rewards and risks, and making strategic moves that have the potential for outsized returns.

While anyone can take a risk, it's important to **minimize the downside**. Billionaires don't just blindly invest; they seek opportunities where they can afford to lose their initial investment, but stand to gain **10X or more** if the opportunity pans out.

5. Leverage Your Network

One of the most powerful tools billionaires use to find 10X opportunities is their **network**. The ultra-wealthy surround themselves with other high-level thinkers, innovators, and entrepreneurs who can help them spot **undiscovered opportunities**. They collaborate, share ideas, and invest together in **game-changing ventures** that have the potential to yield huge returns.

By aligning yourself with the right people and building your own network, you gain access to opportunities that might otherwise be out of reach.

Examples of 10X Opportunities

To truly understand the power of the Law of Asymmetry, let's look at some real-life examples:

- **Early Investors in Facebook**: When Facebook was just a small social network, few could have predicted its rise to become a global platform. Those who invested early saw a **10X** return as the company exploded in value over the years.

- **The Real Estate Boom**: Investors who bought property in emerging markets before they became hotbeds of development have seen massive returns. The key was identifying cities or regions that were **undervalued** but had the potential for rapid growth.

- **Startups and Tech Innovations**: Companies like **Uber, Airbnb**, and **Snapchat** started with small investments but grew exponentially, creating billions in value for early investors.

The Bottom Line: Seeking Asymmetric Opportunities

The Law of Asymmetry is about seeking out opportunities where the **potential reward** far outweighs the **potential risk**. By focusing on high-reward, low-risk investments that have the potential to **10X** your wealth, you put yourself in a position to create massive, life-changing returns. Billionaires don't settle for small wins—they look for **opportunities that have the potential to change everything**. By embracing the Law of Asymmetry, you can start to think bigger, take smarter risks, and position yourself for exponential wealth growth.

The Law of Financial Intelligence: Mastering Money Management

---

One of the most powerful forces driving extreme wealth is **Financial Intelligence**. While many people see money management as something for accountants or financial advisors, the ultra-wealthy understand that mastering your own finances is a **key pillar** of building lasting wealth. The **Law of Financial Intelligence** is about making smart decisions with your money, understanding how money works, and using it as a tool to grow your wealth exponentially.

What Is Financial Intelligence?

At its core, **financial intelligence** is the ability to make informed decisions about your money—where to invest it, how to save it, and how to grow it. It's not just about how much money you make, but about how you **manage, allocate, and grow** that money to generate more wealth over time.

Billionaires understand that wealth isn't just about accumulating money. It's about using that money to make **even more** money. They see money as a tool to fund their goals, not as an end in itself. To truly master wealth, you need to **learn the rules** of how money works and apply them wisely.

Why Financial Intelligence Matters

The rich don't rely solely on earning high incomes—they use **financial intelligence** to maximize the value of every dollar they have. They know that money is a tool, and like any tool, it's only as effective as your ability to use it.

For example, imagine you're working hard at a job and getting paid well. But if you're spending all your earnings on expenses with little to show for it in the long run, you're not managing money effectively. On the other hand, the ultra-wealthy look for ways to make their money **work for them**, multiplying their wealth through **investments, assets**, and strategic financial moves.

Billionaires aren't just good at making money—they are great at managing and growing it. This is what makes the difference between someone who is financially stable and someone who is truly wealthy.

Key Principles of Financial Intelligence

To master the Law of Financial Intelligence, there are several key principles that billionaires live by. These principles don't require a degree in finance—they just require the right mindset and discipline to implement them.

1. Understanding the Difference Between Assets and Liabilities

The first step in financial intelligence is understanding the basic concept of **assets** and **liabilities**. Assets are things that **put money in your pocket**—such as investments, income-generating properties, or businesses. Liabilities, on the other hand, are things that **take money out of your pocket**—like debt, expenses, and anything that doesn't provide an income stream.

Billionaires focus on acquiring **assets** that generate cash flow. This is the key difference between someone who works for money and someone who makes money work for them. By accumulating assets and minimizing liabilities, you set yourself on the path to financial independence and extreme wealth.

2. The Power of Compound Growth

Compound growth is one of the most powerful principles in finance. It's the process of earning money on your money—growing your wealth exponentially over time. The ultra-wealthy understand that **small, consistent investments** over time can turn into **massive amounts of wealth**.

Take, for example, investing in the stock market or buying income-generating real estate. The more you invest, the more you earn from those investments, and the process compounds over time. This is why starting early with investing can lead to huge rewards later. **Time** and **compound interest** are your greatest allies in building wealth.

3. Diversification: Spreading Your Risk

Billionaires understand the importance of **diversification**—spreading their money across different types of investments to reduce risk. Instead of putting all their eggs in one basket, they build a **diverse portfolio** that includes stocks, bonds, real estate, private equity, and even alternative assets like **cryptocurrency**.

By diversifying, they protect themselves from major financial setbacks and ensure that if one investment doesn't perform, others will make up for it. Financial intelligence means knowing where to put your money to get the highest return while balancing the risk.

4. Cash Flow is King

Billionaires focus on creating **consistent cash flow**. While growing wealth is important, the ultra-wealthy prioritize **cash flow** because it allows them to reinvest in their businesses, assets, and investments. Whether it's through **rental**

income, dividends, or business profits, cash flow provides the liquidity necessary to keep growing and scaling.

When you have a steady stream of cash flow, you don't have to rely solely on your earned income from a job. This freedom allows you to pursue new investment opportunities, fund future ventures, and even take on **bigger risks** because you have the cash reserves to back you up.

5. Financial Discipline and Control

Another key aspect of financial intelligence is **discipline**. The rich are often disciplined about their spending, saving, and investing habits. They don't live pay-check to pay-check, and they don't waste money on frivolous expenses. Instead, they follow strict financial plans and budgets that allow them to put their money to work.

Billionaires are masters of **delayed gratification**. Instead of spending all their money on luxuries in the short-term, they choose to invest in their future. They are willing to sacrifice now to reap the rewards later.

6. Taking Calculated Risks

While billionaires are disciplined, they also understand the importance of taking **calculated risks**. They don't gamble recklessly with their money—they do their research, weigh the potential rewards, and make strategic decisions that have the potential for high returns.

Taking risks doesn't mean being careless. It means identifying opportunities where the reward is worth the risk. Whether it's investing in a startup, entering a new market, or launching a new product, billionaires make decisions with confidence because they are well-informed and strategic.

How to Master Your Own Financial Intelligence

Mastering financial intelligence is a journey. It starts with taking control of your money and **educating yourself** about how it works. Here's how to get started:

- **Learn the Basics**: Educate yourself about assets, liabilities, cash flow, and the power of compound growth. The more you understand how money works, the better decisions you can make.

- **Track Your Spending**: Take a close look at your income and expenses. Are you spending more than you earn? Do you have debts draining your resources? Make adjustments to ensure you're in control of your financial future.

- **Invest in Assets**: Start focusing on acquiring assets that can generate income. This could be stocks, real estate, or even starting your own business. Build a portfolio of investments that will work for you.

- **Reinvest Your Earnings**: Instead of spending your earnings, **reinvest them** to create more wealth. Use the power of compound growth to your advantage.

- **Seek Mentorship**: Learn from those who have mastered financial intelligence. Find mentors or advisors who can help you make informed financial decisions.

The Bottom Line: Financial Intelligence Equals Freedom

The Law of Financial Intelligence is about learning how to make money work for you. It's about mastering your finances, understanding the rules of wealth-building, and making smart decisions that grow your wealth over time. By applying these principles, you can break free from the cycle of pay-check-to-pay-check living and move into the realm of true financial freedom. **Master money management, and the money will follow**.

The Law of Purpose: Wealth with Meaning and Impact

While the pursuit of wealth is often seen as a goal in itself, the **Law of Purpose** teaches us that true and lasting wealth is about more than just amassing money. It's about creating wealth that is **meaningful** and leaves a **lasting impact**. This law is based on the principle that **purpose-driven wealth** is wealth that not only enriches your life but also has the power to transform the lives of others.

The Power of Purpose in Building Extreme Wealth

The ultra-wealthy understand that money is a tool, not the ultimate goal. The **true power of wealth** lies in its ability to serve a **greater purpose**. Billionaires don't just build businesses or accumulate assets for personal gain—they do so with the goal of **making a difference**, solving problems, and improving the world around them.

Take, for example, visionary entrepreneurs like **Bill Gates** and **Oprah Winfrey**. While both have amassed incredible fortunes, their true legacy lies in how they have used their wealth to **impact lives**. Gates with his **Bill & Melinda Gates Foundation** and Winfrey with her **Oprah Winfrey Foundation** have channeled their wealth into causes that help people around the world.

This is not by chance. The wealth they've accumulated has been driven by a deeper mission—a purpose that goes beyond personal gain and aligns with their values. Their wealth isn't just about numbers on a balance sheet; it's about creating **meaningful change** that ripples through generations.

Wealth Built on Purpose Is Sustainable Wealth

When your wealth is anchored in a higher purpose, it becomes **sustainable**. This is a key difference between those who make a quick fortune and those who build **generational wealth**. Purpose gives you something deeper to hold onto during hard times, and it can guide your decisions even when the path to wealth gets difficult.

When you build wealth with a sense of purpose, you are more likely to attract people, resources, and opportunities that align with your mission. Purpose-driven wealth tends to multiply because it has the power to inspire and unite others who are passionate about your vision.

The Shift from 'How Much Can I Make?' to 'How Much Impact Can I Create?'

The **Law of Purpose** shifts your mindset from asking, "How much can I make?" to "How much impact can I create?" This shift is critical for anyone looking to build extreme wealth.

Billionaires don't just chase profits—they chase **opportunities to make a difference**. The pursuit of wealth without purpose often leads to burnout, dissatisfaction, and a sense of emptiness. But when wealth is built around a purpose, it becomes **fuel for your passion** and **energy for your mission**.

This mindset shift often leads to greater success, as it helps you identify opportunities that might not be immediately obvious to others. A **purpose-driven business** doesn't just focus on making money—it focuses on providing solutions that people genuinely need. This focus leads to long-term customer loyalty, stronger brands, and greater market value.

Wealth with Purpose Creates a Legacy

When your wealth is tied to a purpose, it creates a legacy that can last for generations. The ultra-wealthy understand that wealth is not just for today but is meant to create **lasting change**. They aim to leave a legacy that impacts **society**, **future generations**, and even **humanity** as a whole.

Think about the wealth that families like the **Rockefellers** and the **Ford family** have created. The wealth they built didn't just provide for their families—it funded **social initiatives**, **educational programs**, and **healthcare projects** that have transformed communities.

The key to creating a meaningful legacy is to ensure that your wealth is aligned with your values. Wealth is not just about what you accumulate—it's about what you give back. Your legacy is not defined by how many zeros are in your bank account but by the **lives you've touched**, the **causes you've supported**, and the **change you've inspired**.

How to Harness the Power of Purpose in Your Wealth Creation

1. **Identify Your Purpose**:

   The first step in the Law of Purpose is to **define your "why"**. What drives you? What is your deeper mission beyond making money? This purpose can be related to a cause, an industry, or a problem you're passionate about solving. Your purpose will guide your actions, investments, and decisions in ways that go beyond just profit.

2. **Build a Business or Investment Strategy Around That Purpose**:

   Once you've identified your purpose, integrate it into your wealth-building strategy. Whether you're launching a business, investing in real estate, or building a portfolio, always ask yourself: **How does this serve my greater purpose?** The best wealth-building ventures are those that provide value to others while allowing you to fulfill your mission.

3. **Align Your Values with Your Investments**:

   The ultra-wealthy understand that their investments should align with their values. Look for opportunities that not only promise financial returns but also have a **positive social impact**. For instance, impact investing, sustainable businesses, or charities that align with your mission can be a great way to multiply your wealth while also contributing to your purpose.

4. **Give Back**:

   Wealth with purpose is not just about creating financial abundance for yourself—it's about creating abundance for others. Consider how you can contribute to the communities, causes, and individuals that align with your values. Philanthropy, whether it's through charitable donations, time, or resources, will multiply the impact of your wealth.

5. **Inspire Others**:

The best way to amplify your purpose-driven wealth is by inspiring others to do the same. Share your mission with others and encourage them to take action. When you lead with purpose, you attract like-minded people who are eager to join your mission, whether it's employees, partners, or customers.

The Bottom Line: Wealth with Meaning is True Wealth

The Law of Purpose teaches us that true wealth is not just about the amount of money you have—it's about the **meaning** and **impact** that wealth creates. When your wealth is aligned with a higher purpose, it's not just a source of financial security but a **tool for transformation**.

By building wealth with purpose, you create a ripple effect that impacts not only your life but also the lives of others. It's a wealth that transcends personal gain and becomes a force for good. And in that pursuit, you'll find that the wealth you accumulate will be far more fulfilling, sustainable, and impactful than any amount of money could ever be on its own.

When you live with purpose, wealth is not just a destination. It's a **journey** toward making a lasting impact on the world around you.

5

The Art of Making Money

Entrepreneurship: Building Scalable Businesses

Entrepreneurship is one of the fastest and most powerful paths to wealth. But what separates those who succeed from those who don't isn't just a great idea—it's the ability to build **scalable businesses**. Scalable businesses are those that can grow significantly without being limited by resources or market size. Simply put, scalability is the key to unlocking massive wealth.

What Makes a Business Scalable?

A scalable business is one that can increase its revenue without a corresponding increase in operational costs. In other words, it's a business that grows **effortlessly** as demand increases. Think about the **tech giants**—companies like **Facebook**, **Amazon**, and **Uber**. These companies started small, but as they expanded, they didn't have to massively increase their resources to keep up with growth. They found ways to **optimize** their operations, using technology, systems, and processes that allowed them to grow **beyond their limitations**.

To create a scalable business, you need to focus on a few key elements:

1. **A Product or Service with High Demand**

   The first step to building a scalable business is having a **product or service** that people **want** and are **willing to pay for**. This could be a tech product, a consumer good, or a service that solves a specific problem. But here's the secret: it's not enough for your product to just be good—it needs to be able to **scale** in the market. Does your product solve a common problem for many people? Does it offer value in a way that makes it **easily marketable** to a wide audience?

2. **The Right Business Model**

   A scalable business relies on a business model that can be replicated quickly and efficiently. This means **low customer acquisition costs** and the ability to reach a broad audience through **automated systems**, **digital marketing**, and **scalable sales processes**. Subscription-based models, for example, are highly scalable because they provide a recurring stream of income without requiring the same amount of work to acquire new customers every time.

3. **Systems and Automation**

   To build a scalable business, you need to set up systems that allow the business to run **smoothly** without requiring your constant attention. This means automating processes where possible—whether it's using software to manage inventory, automating customer communications, or streamlining your financial operations. The less hands-on work you have to do, the easier it is for your business to grow without adding more complexity or costs.

4. **Leverage Technology**

   The wealthiest entrepreneurs use technology as a tool to scale their businesses rapidly. From e-commerce platforms to **cloud-based tools**, leveraging the right technology allows you to run your business more efficiently and reach a wider audience. Think of technology as a multiplier—using the right tech can help you automate your sales, marketing, and operations, which means you don't have to rely on hiring more employees or spending more time to keep up with the growth.

5. **Building a Team and Delegation**

   Even the best entrepreneurs can't do everything on their own. To scale, you need to build a team that can handle various aspects of the business. This doesn't mean hiring dozens of people right away. It means identifying the key roles that will allow your business to grow and finding the right talent to take over those responsibilities. The more you delegate, the more time you have to focus on growing your business, creating new opportunities, and looking for ways to improve your product or service.

Why Entrepreneurship is a Fast Path to Wealth

Entrepreneurship provides the unique opportunity to create something from scratch and turn it into a **highly profitable** business. While it's not without its risks, the rewards for building a successful scalable business are immense. Once your business takes off, the return on investment can be exponential. The **wealthiest entrepreneurs** don't just make money—they **multiply** it by building businesses that can grow and thrive without their constant presence.

In entrepreneurship, you control your destiny. Unlike a traditional job where your income is often tied to the hours you work, entrepreneurship allows you to build something that can **work for you**. Through scalability, automation, and delegation, you can step back from the day-to-day operations and watch your wealth grow.

How to Get Started on Your Path to Scalable Wealth

1. **Identify a Problem and Solve It**

   The best businesses solve a problem that many people face. Whether it's a product, a service, or an innovative solution, your goal as an entrepreneur is to make life easier, better, or more enjoyable for others. The bigger the problem you solve, the more valuable your business becomes.

2. **Think Long-Term**

   Building a scalable business is a long-term game. You're not looking for quick profits or one-off sales. You want to build something that can thrive and grow for years to come. Stay focused on creating value and building a brand that people trust.

3. **Start Small, Think Big**

   Many successful entrepreneurs start small but have big visions. Don't get discouraged if your business starts with limited resources or a small customer base. Focus on building a **solid foundation**, and then look for ways to scale it as demand increases. Your business doesn't need to be massive from day one—it just needs to be **scalable**.

4. **Be Willing to Take Risks**

   Entrepreneurship is inherently risky, but it's also incredibly rewarding. The most successful entrepreneurs are the ones who take calculated risks—investing in growth opportunities, hiring the right talent, and scaling their operations. With the right mindset, risk can be your biggest ally in building wealth.

5. **Focus on Customer Experience**

   Scalable businesses thrive when customers keep coming back. The more value you provide, the more loyal your customer base becomes. **Great customer service**, **user-friendly products**, and **exceptional experiences** keep customers happy and encourage them to refer others, helping your business grow even faster.

The Bottom Line: Entrepreneurship Is the Fastest Path to Extreme Wealth

Building a scalable business is one of the most powerful ways to create extreme wealth. It's not about working harder—it's about working smarter, using technology, systems, and automation to grow your business exponentially. With the right product, business model, and team, you can create a business that doesn't just generate income but **multiplies it**, allowing you to achieve financial freedom and build lasting wealth.

If you're ready to build a business that works for you, start thinking about scalability today. Focus on solving real problems, building systems that allow for growth, and creating a customer experience that keeps people coming back. The wealth will follow.

Investing: Making Your Money Work for You

When it comes to building wealth, **investing** is one of the most powerful tools at your disposal. Unlike earning money through a job or business, investing allows you to **make your money work for you**. Instead of trading your time for cash, investing gives you the opportunity to grow your wealth over time without constantly being involved in the process.

But here's the thing: successful investing is not about gambling or getting lucky—it's about making smart decisions, understanding where your money is going, and being patient enough to let it grow. This is the essence of the billionaire mindset: making your money multiply.

The Basics of Investing

At its core, investing is about purchasing assets that have the potential to **grow in value** over time. These assets could be anything from **stocks**, **bonds**, **real estate**, **businesses**, or even **alternative investments** like **art**, **cryptocurrency**, or **commodities**. The goal is simple: put your money into something that will increase in value and provide you with a return.

But investing isn't a one-size-fits-all approach. There are different types of investments with varying levels of risk, return, and time horizon. To master investing, you need to understand the landscape and decide what works best for your goals.

The Key to Successful Investing: Time

The most important factor in investing is **time**. When you invest, you're giving your money the chance to grow over months, years, and even decades. This process, known as **compound growth**, is one of the most powerful wealth-building tools available. Essentially, your investments earn returns, and then those returns start earning returns as well. Over time, the growth becomes exponential.

For example, let's say you invest $10,000 in the stock market, earning an average of 7% annually. After one year, your investment will be worth $10,700. But the next year, your return is based on $10,700, not just the original $10,000. The longer you leave your money invested, the more it compounds and grows, making the initial amount seem small compared to the long-term result.

The Power of Diversification

One of the biggest mistakes new investors make is putting all their money into one investment. The wealthiest investors understand the importance of **diversification**. This means spreading your money across different types of assets so that if one investment doesn't perform well, you're not left with all your eggs in one basket.

Diversification can happen in many ways:

- **Asset Diversification**: Spread your investments across various asset classes, such as stocks, bonds, real estate, and alternative investments.

- **Sector Diversification**: Invest in different industries—tech, healthcare, real estate, and more—so that your investments are not reliant on one market or sector.

- **Geographical Diversification**: Don't limit yourself to one country or region. Global markets offer opportunities that can help protect your investments against local economic downturns.

By diversifying, you increase the chances that your money will continue to grow, even when one area of the market experiences a slowdown.

Smart Investing vs. Speculating

There's a major difference between **smart investing** and **speculating**. Speculation is when you gamble on an asset, hoping that its price will rise quickly so you can make a fast profit. This approach is risky and often leads to losses when things don't go as planned.

On the other hand, **smart investing** is about making calculated decisions based on thorough research and long-term trends. It's about buying assets that have real value, such as companies with solid growth potential or real estate in high-demand areas.

The wealthiest investors don't chase quick wins or unpredictable markets. They focus on long-term value and steady returns. They look for opportunities that provide both **growth potential** and **stability**, allowing them to accumulate wealth without exposing themselves to unnecessary risk.

The Importance of Education

Successful investing doesn't happen by accident. The wealthiest people understand that in order to make their money work for them, they need to continually educate themselves about the markets and investment opportunities. This doesn't mean you need to become an expert in every investment strategy, but it does mean that you should be **constantly learning** about the different ways to grow your wealth.

Read books, take courses, listen to podcasts, and stay up to date on market trends. The more knowledge you gain, the better equipped you'll be to make informed decisions and avoid common investing mistakes.

Start Where You Are

One of the biggest barriers people face when it comes to investing is the feeling that they need a lot of money to get started. The truth is, you don't need to be wealthy to begin investing. Many investment platforms allow you to start with a small amount of money—sometimes as little as $50 or $100.

The key is to start **now**. The earlier you begin investing, the more time your money has to grow. Even small contributions over time can build into significant wealth.

Remember, building wealth is a marathon, not a sprint. The more you learn, the more you invest, and the more patient you are, the closer you will get to achieving financial freedom.

Conclusion: Let Your Money Work for You

The art of investing is about making your money work as hard as you do. While earning an income through a job or business is important, investing allows you to **build wealth that can outpace your efforts**. By starting early, educating yourself, and choosing the right investments, you can create a **stream of passive income** that continues to grow year after year.

As you master investing, you'll see how your wealth multiplies, giving you the opportunity to achieve financial freedom. And when your money works for you,

you're no longer limited by time. Instead, you've unlocked one of the fastest paths to building lasting wealth and creating the life you've always dreamed of.

Real Estate & Ownership: The Silent Billionaire Strategy

When it comes to building massive wealth, **real estate** has been one of the most reliable and powerful tools used by the world's wealthiest individuals. In fact, **real estate** is often referred to as the "silent billionaire strategy" because it allows individuals to amass significant wealth without the noise and attention that comes with other more flashy methods of making money.

But why is real estate such a consistent wealth builder? The answer lies in the combination of **ownership**, **appreciation**, and the **ability to generate passive income**. The beauty of real estate is that it offers long-term value, stability, and several ways to profit.

Owning vs. Renting: The Wealth Divide

One of the fundamental ways that the wealthy think differently from the average person is in how they view **ownership**. While many people rent their homes or properties, the ultra-wealthy prioritize **owning** real estate.

When you own a property, it's an asset that appreciates over time. Renters, on the other hand, make monthly payments without seeing any return on their money. Homeowners and real estate investors, however, have the potential to make a profit on their properties through **appreciation**—meaning the value of the property increases over time.

Even if the property doesn't immediately increase in value, ownership still provides other advantages. You can rent it out for passive income or improve the property and sell it for a profit. This is the power of **leverage**, a principle that the wealthy understand well. They use other people's money—through loans or partnerships—to build a real estate portfolio that generates income and increases in value without needing all their own cash upfront.

The Power of Appreciation

One of the key reasons real estate has made many people rich is its ability to **appreciate** in value. Unlike most investments, real estate typically increases in value over time, especially in areas with growing populations or strong demand.

For example, if you buy a property today for $200,000, in 10 years, it could be worth $400,000—or more. This increase in value is known as **capital appreciation**, and it's one of the most powerful wealth-building tools available.

However, this doesn't mean that all real estate automatically appreciates. The secret to success lies in **location, location, location**—choosing properties in areas that are likely to see strong growth in demand over the long term. The wealthiest investors know how to identify these areas before they become hotspots, allowing them to profit from the inevitable rise in property values.

Cash Flow: Building Passive Income

While real estate appreciates in value, it can also generate **consistent cash flow**. This is the money that comes in from renting out a property—whether it's a residential home, commercial space, or vacation rental.

The beauty of cash flow is that it allows real estate owners to generate income without having to actively work for it. Once you have tenants in place, the property essentially pays for itself. With the right property, your rent payments can cover the mortgage, taxes, insurance, and maintenance costs, leaving you with extra money each month.

But the real opportunity comes when you own multiple properties or larger assets. Imagine owning several apartment buildings or commercial real estate. As the rents increase over time, so does your cash flow, which can create a steady stream of **passive income** that eventually becomes a significant part of your wealth.

The Power of Leverage in Real Estate

One of the wealthiest secrets in real estate is **leverage**—the ability to use other people's money (typically through loans) to buy properties. This is where the true magic of wealth creation happens.

For example, if you want to buy a $500,000 property, you don't need to pay the entire $500,000 upfront. You can take out a mortgage and pay only a fraction of the property's value—say, 20%. In this case, you would need to come up with $100,000 and borrow the rest.

Even though you only put down $100,000, you still get to enjoy the appreciation and cash flow from the entire $500,000 property. Over time, as the property increases in value, you profit from the full $500,000 worth of growth, not just the portion you invested yourself. This is the power of leverage.

The wealthy understand that by using leverage smartly, they can scale their real estate holdings quickly and create exponential wealth. They're able to own multiple properties without tying up all of their capital, which leaves room for even more investment opportunities.

Real Estate vs. Other Investments

What sets real estate apart from other investments is its ability to provide both **stability and growth**. Stocks can be volatile, and market conditions can change quickly, leaving investors with unpredictable returns. Real estate, on the other hand, tends to move in a more steady and predictable way, especially when it's in the right location.

Additionally, real estate is a **tangible asset**. You can see it, touch it, and improve it. This gives you a sense of control over your investment that stocks or bonds don't provide. If you have a property that isn't performing well, you can fix it, renovate it, or improve its appeal to tenants, increasing its value and profitability.

This combination of stability, appreciation, and control is what makes real estate such an attractive option for wealth-building. For many of the world's billionaires, real estate has been the cornerstone of their wealth.

The Silent Billionaire Strategy: Ownership

The key to the **silent billionaire strategy** lies in **owning** real estate, particularly income-generating properties. Wealthy individuals don't wait for the market to make them rich; they take control of their financial future by accumulating real estate assets that provide them with appreciation, cash flow, and leverage.

While it may seem like a quiet, slow path to wealth, the beauty of real estate is that it **builds wealth steadily** over time. And as you acquire more properties, you unlock the true power of exponential growth—building wealth that continues to grow long after you've made the initial investment.

For those looking to follow in the footsteps of the billionaires, the lesson is clear: **start investing in real estate today**. By doing so, you'll be laying the foundation for long-term wealth that will work for you, even while you sleep. The best time to start is always now, and the silent billionaire strategy of real estate ownership will allow you to create lasting wealth for generations to come.

4o mini

The Digital Economy: New-Age Wealth Creation in Tech and AI

The world is changing faster than ever before, and with it, the ways we create and accumulate wealth. Enter the **Digital Economy**—a thriving ecosystem where the rules of the game are being rewritten by **technology** and **artificial intelligence (AI)**. This new frontier is where some of the most rapid and transformative wealth is being created today. For those who understand how to leverage it, the digital economy offers unprecedented opportunities for growth, scalability, and innovation.

But what exactly is the **digital economy**, and how can you tap into its power? Simply put, it's the economy driven by **digital technologies**, where businesses, products, and services are primarily powered by software, the internet, and AI. This is where **technology** meets **business**, creating new industries, new ways of doing business, and new streams of income that didn't even exist a decade ago.

Tech Startups: Building the Future

In the past, the pathway to wealth was often through traditional industries like real estate, manufacturing, or finance. Today, the fastest way to accumulate extreme wealth is through **tech startups**. These are companies born out of digital innovations—businesses built on the back of cutting-edge software, cloud computing, or AI technologies.

What makes tech startups so powerful is their **scalability**. With a solid business model and a good product, a tech company can grow quickly without needing to increase its costs in the same proportion. This scalability allows startups to achieve massive growth, sometimes within a few years. For example, companies like **Facebook**, **Uber**, and **Airbnb** went from startups to billion-dollar companies in record time, creating immense wealth for their founders and investors.

The digital economy enables individuals to start businesses with relatively low capital investment compared to traditional industries. You don't need to build factories or inventory. With the right idea, all you need is a laptop, some coding skills (or the right team), and the ability to scale. Whether it's launching a software-as-a-service (SaaS) product, creating an app, or developing an online platform, the opportunities for digital entrepreneurship are endless.

Artificial Intelligence: The New Gold Rush

In the same way the Industrial Revolution fueled the rise of wealth through manufacturing, **artificial intelligence (AI)** is driving the new wealth revolution. AI isn't just a buzzword—it's a game-changer. From **machine learning** to **predictive analytics**, AI has the potential to transform industries, create new markets, and unlock profits in ways we never thought possible.

The wealthiest people in the world, such as **Elon Musk**, **Jeff Bezos**, and **Mark Zuckerberg**, are investing heavily in AI technologies. Why? Because AI has the power to **automate tasks**, **improve efficiency**, and **deliver superior products and services** that customers crave. And it doesn't stop there—AI is revolutionizing everything from healthcare to finance to entertainment.

For anyone serious about wealth creation, understanding and harnessing AI is key. Whether you're developing AI tools, investing in AI companies, or using AI to streamline your own business operations, the opportunities are vast. **Machine learning algorithms** are now being used to predict market trends, optimize advertising, personalize customer experiences, and even create art. AI is pushing the boundaries of what's possible, and those who invest in it will be the ones reaping the rewards.

The Power of Automation and Passive Income

One of the greatest advantages of the digital economy is **automation**. In the past, wealth creation often required constant effort—long hours at a desk, running a physical store, or managing employees. In the digital economy, however, technology allows you to **automate** much of the work.

For example, think about **affiliate marketing**, **digital products**, or **online courses**. Once you've created a digital product or service, you can automate its delivery. This means you can continue making money without having to constantly work. You might spend a few hours creating the product or setting up the system, but once it's live, it can generate **passive income** for you while you sleep.

The digital economy is also home to **platform businesses**—companies like **Amazon**, **Shopify**, and **Etsy** that allow individuals to set up shop online and sell products or services to millions of customers around the world. These platforms offer built-in traffic and tools to help you scale your business without the need for heavy upfront costs.

The Global Market: Access to Billions

Another advantage of the digital economy is that it provides **global access**. In the past, businesses were limited to serving customers within a specific geographic area, but with the rise of the internet and digital platforms, companies can now reach customers anywhere on the planet.

This **global reach** means you're no longer confined to your local market. Whether you're offering a digital product, providing a service, or selling physical goods, the entire world becomes your potential customer base. This level of access creates endless opportunities for scaling your business to unimaginable heights.

You're no longer competing with just the local companies around you—you're competing in a global marketplace. The opportunity for wealth creation is exponentially larger when you have access to billions of people online.

Investment Opportunities in the Digital Economy

The digital economy also offers a wealth of **investment opportunities**. You don't need to be a billionaire to tap into the tech world. Today, there are plenty of ways for average investors to get involved, from **buying stocks** in tech companies to investing in **cryptocurrencies** or **tech startups**.

For those looking to create wealth through investing, the digital space is ripe with opportunities. **Blockchain**, **cryptocurrency**, and **FinTech** are all industries that are quickly growing and evolving, presenting incredible returns for early investors. And even in traditional tech companies, such as those focused on **cloud computing**, **software**, and **cybersecurity**, there's massive upside potential.

Conclusion: Embrace the Digital Revolution

The digital economy is reshaping how wealth is created, and **technology** and **AI** are at the heart of it. Whether you're building a startup, investing in tech, or automating your business, the opportunities are abundant for those who are ready to embrace this new age of wealth creation.

The richest people in the world are not just using technology—they are creating it, investing in it, and leveraging it to scale their wealth. **The digital economy is the fastest path to wealth today**, and the sooner you tap into it, the sooner you can unlock the limitless potential it offers.

As the digital revolution continues to unfold, it's time to get ahead of the curve. Learn, innovate, invest, and create. This is the future of wealth creation, and it's waiting for you.

6

Passive Income – Make Money While Sleeping

The Myth of Passive Income: What Really Works

It's a dream that's been sold to us a thousand times: **passive income**. The idea that you can make money while you sleep, without lifting a finger. Who wouldn't want that? Picture this: you wake up in the morning, check your bank account, and see that money has been deposited while you were fast asleep. It sounds like the perfect setup, doesn't it?

The reality, however, is not as simple as the myth suggests. The truth is, **passive income** is rarely "completely passive." While it's entirely possible to generate income streams that require minimal ongoing effort, they still need careful planning, attention, and sometimes a bit of active work upfront.

So, let's break down the myth and get to what really works when it comes to creating passive income.

The Real Deal with Passive Income

Real passive income doesn't mean you just sit back and watch money roll in. It involves building systems that can generate income with as little effort as possible after they're set up. And setting up these systems is the key to long-term success.

Here are some examples of income streams that *can* become relatively passive over time:

1. **Rental Income**: Owning real estate and renting it out is one of the oldest forms of passive income. However, being a landlord isn't entirely passive. You'll need to manage the property, handle repairs, and deal with tenants. That said, if you hire property managers, your role can be reduced significantly.

2. **Dividends from Investments**: Investing in stocks or bonds that pay dividends is another example of passive income. You earn money from your investments without selling them. But there's a catch—choosing the right investments, monitoring them, and understanding market trends is still important to ensure consistent returns.

3. **Royalties from Creative Work**: Authors, musicians, and inventors can earn royalties from their creations. Once a book, song, or patent is created, it can continue generating income without ongoing effort. However, the creation of the work itself requires significant time, energy, and skill.

4. **Online Businesses and Digital Products**: You can create products like online courses, e-books, or software that can be sold repeatedly with little to no ongoing effort. However, the initial work of creating the product, setting up an online sales funnel, and marketing it effectively is where the work happens. Once those systems are in place, they can run with minimal day-to-day input.

The Key Ingredient: Hard Work Upfront

No matter what kind of passive income stream you're pursuing, the secret to success lies in **hard work upfront**. The idea that you can create something once and forget about it is an illusion. Yes, many passive income sources require less time once they're set up, but getting there isn't automatic.

For example, creating an online business might seem like a set-and-forget type of endeavor, but the truth is it will take hours, days, and perhaps even months of work to get everything running smoothly. You'll need to develop a product, find customers, build a website, and market your business—just to name a few. But once you've done that and established a solid system, the income may flow in with less effort.

Active and Passive Income Are Partners, Not Opponents

Here's an important thing to keep in mind: **active income** and **passive income** are not enemies—they can actually work hand in hand. Building an active income stream (like working a job or running a business) can help you fund the creation of passive income. Think of it this way: active income can give you the capital to invest in real estate, stocks, or other passive income projects.

Over time, once these passive systems are established, they can give you the freedom to scale back your active work, but **it's unlikely that you'll go from 0 to 100% passive income immediately**. Instead, think of passive income as a long-term project that requires steady effort and strategic planning to make it sustainable.

Beware of "Get Rich Quick" Schemes

There's no shortage of people who promise to teach you how to make passive income quickly, and they often present overly simplistic or downright deceptive methods. Beware of **"get-rich-quick" schemes** that promise you'll make money effortlessly. These often don't deliver real value and may even cost you more than you make in the long run.

The best approach is to **build your passive income streams slowly and strategically**. Focus on creating long-term value, and the returns will follow. This process will require both patience and persistence, but the rewards will be worth it in the end.

The Bottom Line: Is Passive Income Worth It?

Absolutely. But don't fall for the myth that it's all smooth sailing. The truth is, building reliable passive income requires hard work, smart planning, and a lot of hustle upfront. But the payoff can be immense.

The key is to set realistic expectations and be prepared to put in the work. Once your systems are in place and running, you'll find yourself with more time and financial freedom. But remember: success doesn't happen overnight, and passive income doesn't mean no work at all—it means smarter work, with the potential for long-term, sustainable wealth.

In the end, creating passive income is less about finding an easy shortcut and more about **creating systems that can work for you**, even when you're not actively involved. And when you get it right, those systems can become the foundation for the wealth you've always dreamed of—slowly, steadily, but with massive results.

Income Streams of the Ultra-Wealthy

When it comes to building extreme wealth, the ultra-wealthy have one thing in common: they don't rely on a single income stream. They understand that wealth grows when money is working for them in multiple ways. For the richest people, income isn't just earned from a salary or a business they run—it comes from **diversified assets** that create income in various forms.

Let's dive into the primary income streams that ultra-wealthy individuals use to accelerate their wealth.

1. Investments in Stocks and Bonds

One of the most common ways the ultra-wealthy make money is through **investments**. They don't just invest for the sake of investing—they focus on **building portfolios** that can generate consistent returns over time.

While regular investors may stick to traditional stocks, bonds, or mutual funds, the ultra-wealthy usually have **well-researched investment strategies**. They diversify across multiple sectors, including real estate, technology, private equity, and even international markets. This allows them to reduce risk while increasing their chances for higher returns.

2. Real Estate and Property Ownership

Real estate is often called the **silent billionaire strategy** because of its ability to generate consistent income while also appreciating in value. The ultra-wealthy buy and hold properties that provide both **rental income** and long-term capital gains.

What makes their strategy different? They invest in **premium locations**, acquire high-end commercial properties, and often leverage **tax benefits** associated with real estate ownership. While many people think of real estate as a passive investment, the ultra-wealthy often treat it as a key part of their active wealth-building strategy, constantly looking for new opportunities in this sector.

3. Business Ventures and Equity Stakes

Starting and scaling businesses is a hallmark of wealth creation. The ultra-wealthy are known for building companies or investing in startups with massive growth potential. They don't just operate businesses; they **own businesses**, often in industries they have expertise or passion in.

They typically take **equity stakes** in businesses—this means they own a portion of the company and benefit from the profits and growth. These businesses, whether tech startups or established companies, act as **income-generating machines** that provide the wealthy with ongoing cash flow.

In some cases, they also act as **angel investors** or venture capitalists, providing early-stage funding to promising startups. This allows them to capitalize on huge potential gains if the company succeeds, while also diversifying their income.

4. Intellectual Property and Royalties

Another income stream for the ultra-wealthy comes from **intellectual property**. Whether it's patents, trademarks, copyrights, or royalties, these assets can generate consistent income without much ongoing effort.

The ultra-wealthy often own the rights to books, music, inventions, and software that continue to produce royalties year after year. For example, famous authors, musicians, and inventors can continue to earn income long after the original creation has been made. This is often seen in the world of **entertainment**, but it applies to many fields, including technology and innovation.

5. Private Equity and Venture Capital

The ultra-wealthy often have a strong presence in **private equity** and **venture capital**. These involve taking equity stakes in private companies (often early-stage or growing companies) in exchange for capital.

Through private equity investments, wealthy individuals often become involved in the strategic direction of the business. They may even offer mentorship or connections to accelerate the company's growth. As these companies scale, the ultra-wealthy see substantial returns on their investments—often with much higher growth potential than traditional stock market investments.

6. Art, Collectibles, and Other Tangible Assets

High-value **art**, rare collectibles, and other tangible assets are another way the ultra-wealthy grow their wealth. While these assets may seem like luxury items, many of them appreciate over time, offering a unique form of **long-term investment**.

Rare art pieces, vintage cars, and even classic wines can become valuable commodities that appreciate in value as time passes. The ultra-wealthy use these assets as both a way to store wealth and an opportunity to diversify their portfolios. It's a form of investing that's less correlated to the stock market, which helps to protect against volatility.

7. Digital Assets: Cryptocurrency and Online Ventures

As the world has become more digital, the ultra-wealthy have started to explore the world of **cryptocurrency** and **digital assets**. Though this is a newer avenue, cryptocurrencies like Bitcoin, Ethereum, and NFTs have become important tools for diversifying portfolios.

The ultra-wealthy are not just buying and holding cryptocurrencies—they're also investing in blockchain technology, developing platforms, or even starting **digital businesses**. Digital assets can provide massive returns, but the ultra-wealthy are strategic in their investments, ensuring they understand the risks and rewards before diving in.

8. Passive Income Streams: Dividends and Interest

Once they've accumulated enough wealth, the ultra-wealthy can create income streams from **passive investments** that provide cash flow without much ongoing effort. This includes **dividends** from stocks, interest from bonds, and returns on various types of savings and investment products.

The key here is that they've already built up enough wealth to where these passive income streams can sustain their lifestyle and fund future investments. This is where **compounding** comes into play—growing wealth at an exponential rate over time.

9. Strategic Partnerships and Joint Ventures

In addition to direct investments, the ultra-wealthy also leverage **strategic partnerships** and **joint ventures** to multiply their income. They team up with other wealthy individuals, corporations, or private investors to fund and manage projects. By pooling resources, they gain access to larger opportunities that they couldn't tackle alone.

Whether it's building large-scale real estate developments or funding multi-million-dollar infrastructure projects, these partnerships allow for exponential growth with shared risk.

Final Thoughts: Diversification is the Key

The ultra-wealthy understand that the best way to create sustainable wealth is through **diversification**. They don't rely on just one income stream; they spread their wealth across various assets and opportunities.

For you, the lesson is clear: **Don't put all your eggs in one basket.** Build multiple income streams—whether through investments, businesses, real estate, or intellectual property—so that your money works for you in different ways.

The faster you start thinking like the ultra-wealthy and diversify your income streams, the closer you'll be to achieving financial freedom and extreme wealth.

Automating and Scaling Your Passive Income Strategy

One of the most powerful concepts for building wealth is the ability to make money while you sleep. This is the magic of **passive income**—earning money without constant effort. But the real secret to unlocking lasting wealth lies not just in earning passive income, but in **automating and scaling** your passive income strategy.

To truly build financial freedom, you need systems that work for you around the clock. The ultra-wealthy have mastered the art of leveraging time, money, and resources to automate their income streams. Let's explore how you can do the same.

1. Leverage Technology to Streamline Processes

The first step in automating your passive income is harnessing the power of **technology**. Whether it's setting up an online business, creating a subscription-based service, or managing investments, technology allows you to work smarter, not harder.

For example, if you're creating an online course or writing an e-book, once it's created, technology can help you sell it automatically. Tools like **automated email sequences**, **sales funnels**, and **shopping cart software** can ensure your business continues to generate revenue 24/7. These tools take care of everything from payment processing to customer follow-up, leaving you free to focus on other projects.

If you're investing in real estate, platforms like **real estate syndication platforms** or property management software can automate rental management, tenant communications, and even payments. The more you integrate tech into your strategy, the less time and effort you need to spend managing it.

2. Create Systems That Run Without You

Building a successful passive income stream means setting up **systems** that operate without constant input from you. Think about businesses or investments that run on **auto-pilot**.

One example is building a **franchise system**. While it may take significant upfront effort, once set up, a franchise can allow you to collect royalties or management fees without having to manage each individual location. Similarly, creating a **self-sustaining online business**—like an affiliate marketing website or dropshipping store—requires initial setup, but once it's running, you can generate sales automatically through search engine traffic or paid ads.

This principle also applies to **investment portfolios**. Rather than manually picking individual stocks or bonds, consider working with robo-advisors or automated investment tools that rebalance your portfolio, select assets, and reinvest profits for you.

3. Outsource and Delegate Responsibilities

One of the most efficient ways to scale your passive income strategy is by learning to **delegate**. While automation handles the technical side, outsourcing frees you up to focus on scaling your business or expanding your investments.

For instance, if you're building an online business, consider hiring virtual assistants to manage customer service, content creation, or social media. By outsourcing the day-to-day tasks, you can focus on growing your revenue streams and exploring new opportunities.

In real estate, you can outsource the property management to a firm that handles tenant screening, maintenance, and rent collection. This allows you to own multiple properties without being bogged down by the daily operations.

By removing yourself from the routine tasks, you free up your time for high-level decision-making and scaling efforts.

4. Build Recurring Revenue Streams

One of the most powerful ways to scale passive income is by focusing on **recurring revenue**. This is income that continues to come in on a regular basis, often with minimal effort. Think of subscription models like **software as a service (SaaS)**, **membership sites**, or **subscription box services**.

These models provide predictable cash flow because customers are charged on a monthly or yearly basis. Once you've established a strong customer base, your income continues to flow without having to constantly make new sales.

Additionally, you can create recurring income from investments such as **dividends** from stocks, **interest** from bonds, or even **royalties** from intellectual property. The beauty of these passive streams is that they grow and compound over time, providing you with increasing wealth without extra work.

5. Scale Through Strategic Partnerships

While automation and delegation are crucial, scaling passive income often requires **strategic partnerships**. Whether it's teaming up with other entrepreneurs, co-investing in projects, or partnering with tech platforms, collaboration can accelerate your growth.

For example, if you're investing in real estate, you might partner with someone who has access to capital, while you bring in expertise in managing properties or finding deals. These kinds of partnerships allow you to scale faster than you could on your own.

In the online business world, you can collaborate with **affiliate marketers** or **influencers** who will help promote your products in exchange for a commission. By tapping into their audiences, you can rapidly expand your reach and increase sales without significant investment.

6. Optimize and Reinforce Your Systems

Once you have a passive income system in place, it's crucial to continuously **optimize and improve** it. This can involve automating more parts of the business, tweaking your marketing strategy, or diversifying into new income streams.

For example, if you're running an online business, you might refine your sales funnel to increase conversions, or use analytics tools to identify areas where you can improve efficiency. If you're investing in stocks or real estate, regularly reviewing and adjusting your portfolio ensures you're capturing the highest returns with the least effort.

By reinforcing your systems with ongoing improvements, you'll ensure that your passive income continues to scale over time, freeing you from day-to-day management while your wealth grows exponentially.

Conclusion: The Power of Automating and Scaling

Automating and scaling your passive income strategy is the key to building wealth without being chained to a desk. The ultra-wealthy don't just work hard—they work smart. By leveraging technology, creating self-sustaining systems, outsourcing tasks, building recurring revenue, forming strategic partnerships, and constantly optimizing, you can create income streams that generate wealth for you while you focus on new opportunities.

Remember, the faster you automate and scale, the quicker you can achieve the financial freedom to live life on your terms. The path to wealth isn't about working harder—it's about working smarter, and leveraging the power of systems to make money work for you.

The 'Invisible Wealth' of Smart Investments

When most people think of wealth, they envision stacks of cash, luxury cars, or grand mansions. But the truly wealthy know that the real treasure lies in what they don't see right away—the **invisible wealth** that comes from smart investments.

Invisible wealth doesn't scream for attention. It isn't flashy. But it grows silently in the background, compounding year after year, often with minimal effort from its owner. These are the investments that build a foundation for long-term financial freedom. While many chase the excitement of fast money, the ultra-wealthy understand that it's the **strategic, steady, and well-planned investments** that create lasting wealth.

Let's explore the concept of invisible wealth and how smart investments can grow it.

1. The Power of Compounding

At the core of invisible wealth is the idea of **compounding**—where your money works for you, growing exponentially over time. This principle is often referred to as the "eighth wonder of the world" because of its immense ability to turn small amounts of money into large sums, if given enough time.

For example, imagine you invest $1,000 in an asset that returns 8% annually. After one year, you'll have $1,080. While that's a small gain, what's powerful is that the next year's 8% will be applied to the new total, $1,080, not just the original $1,000. Over time, this compounding effect turns modest investments into significant wealth, often without requiring active involvement. The wealthy embrace this long-term growth, knowing it's how wealth accumulates silently, away from the public eye.

2. Real Estate: The Invisible Asset

Real estate is one of the oldest and most powerful forms of smart investment that quietly builds invisible wealth. The ultra-wealthy often invest in properties that **appreciate** in value over time, generating passive income while they sleep.

Let's say you buy a property for $200,000. In the early years, your focus may be on collecting rent. But as time passes, the value of that property increases, often significantly. Meanwhile, the rent you collect may cover the mortgage, taxes, and maintenance costs, leaving you with little out-of-pocket expense. Over time, as the property appreciates and your loan balance decreases, your equity grows, increasing your wealth—quietly and without fanfare.

This combination of appreciation and rental income can add up to invisible wealth that steadily grows in the background, requiring little active effort once the investment is made.

3. The Magic of Stock Market Investments

Another key element of invisible wealth is **stock market investments**—particularly long-term investments in stocks, bonds, or mutual funds. While stock market investing may seem risky to some, the reality is that the stock market has historically delivered strong returns over time. Those who invest wisely in stocks, particularly **dividend-paying stocks** or **index funds**, can build invisible wealth.

Let's say you invest in a well-established company that pays regular dividends. Initially, the dividend may seem modest, but over time, these payouts accumulate, and the reinvestment of dividends can further compound your returns. In addition to dividends, the stock may also appreciate in value, contributing to your invisible wealth.

In contrast to the quick gains often associated with speculative trading, this strategy builds wealth slowly and steadily, often without any immediate, visible rewards. But over time, it quietly creates financial independence.

4. Intellectual Property and Royalties

Another form of invisible wealth is tied to **intellectual property (IP)**, such as patents, trademarks, copyrights, or even creative works like books, music, or inventions. While many think of royalties as small payments, the wealth they generate over time is powerful.

Take the example of an author who writes a best-selling book. Initially, the income from book sales may seem modest, but as the book continues to sell over time, the royalties build up. This passive income continues to flow to the author long after the book was first published. Similarly, a musician may earn royalties for years from a song they created decades ago. These streams of passive income are the hallmark of invisible wealth—quietly growing and accumulating wealth without much effort from the owner.

5. Automating Income Streams

Invisible wealth is also created through the automation of income streams. Think of **online businesses**, such as e-commerce stores or automated digital products, like online courses or memberships. Once set up, these systems can generate revenue with little ongoing involvement.

For example, an online course that you create today can continue to sell year after year. If properly marketed and optimized, it may run on autopilot—constantly bringing in sales, without any active participation. The real beauty of this invisible wealth lies in its ability to generate income while you focus on other projects or enjoy life.

6. Building Wealth Through Smart Risk-Taking

Invisible wealth is often built through **smart risks**—investments that may seem unexciting at first but prove highly lucrative over time. Think about investing in early-stage startups, cryptocurrencies, or alternative assets like fine art or wine. These types of investments may carry risk, but they also offer the potential for high returns that are invisible at the start.

For example, early investments in tech companies like Apple or Amazon seemed risky at the time but have now created massive wealth for those who took the chance. The key to these investments is **patience**—allowing the investment to mature and grow over time, without panicking at the short-term fluctuations.

7. The Importance of Patience and Long-Term Vision

Ultimately, invisible wealth is about **thinking long-term**. The wealthy understand that creating lasting wealth isn't about quick wins, but about building assets that grow steadily, often without immediate visibility. It's about planting seeds today and allowing them to grow quietly in the background, with the potential to pay off in the years and decades to come.

Smart investments build invisible wealth because they accumulate over time, requiring little ongoing effort. The longer you stay invested, the more your wealth compounds. As your assets grow and diversify, you're creating a financial future that thrives silently behind the scenes—until, one day, you look up and realize just how much you've accumulated.

Conclusion: The Silent Power of Smart Investments

Invisible wealth is the cornerstone of financial freedom. It grows in the background, often unnoticed, but the impact is profound. Whether through compounding investments, real estate, stocks, intellectual property, or other smart strategies, the key is to make investments today that will generate income tomorrow—and for years to come.

This kind of wealth doesn't demand constant attention, flashy displays, or quick results. Instead, it builds over time, and in the end, it's far more powerful than the most visible forms of wealth. The ultra-wealthy know this secret—they understand the power of invisible wealth and use it to build their empires, quietly and steadily. And now, you know the secret, too.

7

The Wealth Multiplication Formula

The Science of Scaling: How to Multiply Your Earnings

Scaling your income isn't just about working harder or adding more hours to your day. It's about working smarter, leveraging your strengths, and multiplying the impact of your efforts. The science of scaling is all about creating systems, automating processes, and building foundations that allow your wealth to grow exponentially.

The idea is simple: instead of relying on your personal time or effort to generate income, you create models that make money work for you, often without your constant involvement. Think of scaling as setting up a machine that runs on its own, where your role becomes more about overseeing the system and ensuring it continues to function smoothly.

Let's break down the steps involved in scaling and multiplying your earnings.

1. Create Systems That Work Without You

The first step to scaling is to create **systems**—reliable, repeatable processes that work without your constant oversight. Think of it like creating a business that runs on autopilot. For example, if you're running an online store, your system might include a website, automated payment processing, inventory management, and customer service that can operate 24/7, even when you're sleeping.

Systems can be applied to almost any income-generating activity. Whether it's a product, service, or investment, find ways to streamline the process. Automation tools, like software for email marketing or managing finances, can reduce the amount of time you spend on repetitive tasks, freeing up your time for more strategic activities.

2. Leverage Other People's Efforts

One of the most powerful ways to scale your earnings is by **leveraging other people's efforts**. This doesn't mean simply delegating tasks—it's about using others to multiply your reach and output. For example, when you hire employees, contractors, or partners, you gain access to their skills and time, allowing you to expand faster than if you were working alone.

In business, this is often referred to as creating a **team of high performers** who can take ownership of different aspects of the business. In essence, you're building a network of people who contribute to your success, all while you focus on scaling the bigger picture.

3. Multiply Through Technology and Tools

In today's world, **technology is a game changer** for scaling your income. The right tools and platforms can help you reach a massive audience, process transactions, and deliver products or services with minimal effort on your part. Whether it's using an e-commerce platform to sell products globally or leveraging social media to create a following, technology can give you the leverage needed to scale quickly and efficiently.

In many cases, technology can replace the need for manual work or hiring more people. For example, a well-designed website can automate sales, and AI-powered chatbots can handle customer service inquiries. By incorporating technology into your business, you free yourself from having to manage every small detail, while simultaneously increasing your capacity to serve more customers.

4. Focus on High-Impact, High-Return Activities

As you scale, you need to be very selective about where you invest your time. It's crucial to focus on the activities that have the **highest impact** and the **highest return**. These are often the tasks that will directly lead to exponential growth.

For example, instead of spending hours on low-level tasks that don't move the needle, spend more time on activities like creating valuable content, making key business partnerships, or identifying new opportunities for growth. These activities have a **multiplier effect**, meaning they can lead to a much larger increase in earnings than the time you invest in them.

5. Reinvest Earnings into Growth

To scale, you need to continuously **reinvest** your earnings into further growth. This could mean hiring more people, launching new products, or investing in marketing to reach more customers. The idea is to treat your earnings not as a personal windfall, but as fuel for the fire of growth.

By reinvesting in your business or investments, you're compounding your success. The more you reinvest, the more your systems, people, and technology can scale, and the faster your income will grow. It's important to have a plan for reinvestment and focus on opportunities that will give you the greatest return on investment (ROI).

6. Create Passive Income Streams

While active income—where you exchange time for money—is essential for building your wealth initially, true scaling happens when you focus on creating **passive income streams**. Passive income allows you to earn money while you sleep or travel, without the need for constant effort.

Real estate investments, royalties from intellectual property, dividend-paying stocks, and online businesses are some examples of passive income sources. Once you set them up, these income streams work for you, earning money without you having to be involved on a daily basis.

The key is to create assets that generate income regularly, and over time, these passive income streams will multiply and grow exponentially. By reinvesting these earnings back into more assets, you further compound your wealth.

7. Think Bigger: The Power of Strategic Expansion

The final step in scaling your income is **thinking bigger**. Once you've established a strong foundation and systems, it's time to look at ways to expand.

This could mean entering new markets, launching new products or services, or even exploring new industries.

Strategic expansion allows you to tap into **new revenue streams** and create additional layers of wealth. It's important to identify opportunities that align with your strengths and resources and then move quickly to capitalize on them.

8. Monitor and Adjust for Maximum Efficiency

Once you've set up systems for scaling, your role becomes one of **overseeing and refining**. Monitor your progress regularly and identify areas for improvement. Scaling isn't a set-it-and-forget-it process. It requires constant monitoring to ensure everything is running smoothly and efficiently.

As you scale, be open to feedback and willing to adjust your strategy as needed. The more you fine-tune your approach, the more efficient and profitable it becomes.

Conclusion: Multiplying Your Earnings

Scaling your income isn't about doing more of the same. It's about working smarter, creating systems that allow your money to grow automatically, leveraging other people and technology, and reinvesting in opportunities that will fuel future growth.

By thinking strategically, focusing on high-impact activities, and embracing passive income, you can create a snowball effect that exponentially multiplies your earnings. And remember—this isn't a quick fix, but a long-term process of building systems and assets that continue to work for you, even when you're not working at all.

If you want to multiply your wealth, start today by implementing these scaling strategies and watch how your earnings grow, compound, and multiply over time.

The Art of Deal-Making & Negotiation

Deal-making is a crucial skill for anyone who wants to multiply their wealth. Whether you're negotiating the sale of a business, closing a real estate deal, or forming a partnership, the ability to strike the right deal is what sets the ultra-wealthy apart from the rest. It's not just about getting the best price or the best terms—it's about creating opportunities that allow both parties to win, and in doing so, generating value that continues to grow over time.

In this chapter, we'll dive into the art of deal-making and negotiation, breaking it down into practical strategies that you can apply to scale your income and multiply your wealth.

1. Understand the Power of Leverage

At the heart of every successful deal is leverage. Leverage is the ability to maximize the value of your resources while minimizing your risk. In business, leverage can come in many forms: financial leverage (using borrowed money), operational leverage (scaling systems and processes), and human leverage (working with skilled partners or employees).

When negotiating, the wealthiest individuals understand the importance of creating deals where they can use leverage to their advantage. By securing favorable terms—whether it's access to capital, valuable partnerships, or favorable contracts—they position themselves to grow their wealth quickly with minimal risk. The more leverage you have, the better deals you can make.

2. Win-Win Deals: Creating Value for Everyone

The most successful negotiators don't aim for a "win-lose" outcome. Instead, they aim for a "win-win" deal—one where all parties walk away feeling like they've gained something valuable. This is the key to building long-term relationships and creating opportunities that pay off well into the future.

Ask yourself, "How can I create a deal where everyone benefits?" This doesn't mean giving up your interests—it means thinking creatively about how to align your goals with those of the other party. For example, in a business partnership, you might negotiate for a bigger equity stake, but in return, you offer unique expertise, access to your network, or valuable assets that the other party needs.

When you think in terms of creating value for all sides, you're more likely to build strong, lasting partnerships that will continue to multiply your wealth over time.

3. Prepare Like a Pro

Preparation is the foundation of every great deal. The more prepared you are, the more confidently you can enter negotiations, and the better your chances of striking a favorable deal. Preparation involves understanding not only what you want from the deal but also what the other party wants. It's about understanding their pain points, needs, and objectives.

In addition, successful negotiators take the time to know the details of the deal inside and out. What are the key terms? What's the timeline? What risks are involved? What's your best alternative if the deal doesn't go through? By preparing thoroughly, you'll be in a better position to navigate the negotiation with clarity and confidence.

4. The Art of Timing

Timing can make or break a deal. The best negotiators understand that **timing is everything**—knowing when to push for a deal, when to hold back, and when to walk away. Often, it's about waiting for the right moment when the other party is most receptive to your terms. This requires patience, intuition, and experience.

The wealthiest individuals also know how to time their moves strategically. They don't jump into deals hastily or under pressure. Instead, they wait for the right moment—when the conditions are optimal. The ability to wait for the perfect timing, combined with the confidence to act when necessary, is what gives the ultra-wealthy an edge in deal-making.

5. Build Relationships, Not Just Deals

While closing a deal is important, building relationships is what creates long-term success. Many successful deal-makers view negotiations as an opportunity to **build trust** and **strengthen relationships**. The goal isn't just to walk away with a signed contract; it's about creating a foundation for future collaboration and opportunities.

By fostering positive relationships with the people you negotiate with, you ensure that your deals lead to more deals in the future. Being respectful, empathetic, and understanding of the other party's needs goes a long way in ensuring that your negotiation isn't just a one-time transaction—it becomes the beginning of a profitable, long-term partnership.

6. Know When to Walk Away

One of the hardest things in negotiation is knowing when to walk away. But understanding when to cut your losses and exit a deal is critical. Wealthy individuals aren't afraid to say "no" when the deal isn't right for them. They know that there will always be other opportunities, and they refuse to settle for terms that don't align with their vision or values.

Learning to walk away is a sign of strength, not weakness. It shows that you're not desperate for a deal but rather focused on building the right deals that align with your long-term goals.

7. Use Data and Facts to Back Your Arguments

When negotiating, emotion can cloud judgment. That's why the most effective deal-makers use **data** and **facts** to support their position. Having solid evidence and numbers on your side gives you credibility and strengthens your argument.

For example, if you're negotiating the price of an asset, come prepared with market data, past performance, and projections to justify your offer. Being able to back up your position with hard facts makes you more persuasive and demonstrates that you're not just negotiating out of personal desire—you're doing it based on solid analysis.

8. The Power of Silence

Sometimes, the most powerful tool in negotiation is silence. When you ask for a concession or present an offer, sometimes the best strategy is to **stay silent** and let the other party fill the gap. Silence creates pressure, and often, the other party will be eager to speak up and offer more favorable terms just to break the silence.

By controlling the flow of conversation and using silence strategically, you put yourself in a position of power during the negotiation.

9. Negotiating for Long-Term Success

In the world of deal-making, it's easy to focus on the immediate gains. But the wealthiest individuals know that **long-term success** is what matters most. Every deal is an opportunity to set up future opportunities—whether it's a partnership that leads to new ventures, or an acquisition that opens the door to new markets.

When negotiating, keep the long-term impact of the deal in mind. Will this opportunity grow over time? Does it align with your ultimate vision? Successful deal-makers think several steps ahead, ensuring that every agreement they make is a stepping stone to greater wealth and influence.

Conclusion: Mastering the Art of Deal-Making

Mastering the art of deal-making and negotiation is about more than just getting the best price or securing favorable terms. It's about creating long-lasting value, building strong relationships, and using strategy and leverage to multiply your wealth. When you approach negotiations with preparation, patience, and the ability to think long-term, you'll be in a much stronger position to make deals that fuel your financial growth.

So, next time you enter a negotiation, remember: It's not just about the deal at hand—it's about the opportunities you're creating for your future.

Partnering with the Right People to Accelerate Growth

One of the most powerful strategies for scaling your income and multiplying your wealth is simple: **partner with the right people**. While it may sound basic, this concept lies at the core of how the ultra-wealthy accelerate their businesses, investments, and ventures to new heights. Success in business isn't just about what you can do on your own—it's about who you align yourself with and how those relationships create exponential opportunities.

In this section, we'll explore why the right partnerships are a game changer, how to identify the best partners, and how these relationships can propel your growth.

The Power of Collaboration

Entrepreneurship is not a solo sport. No matter how skilled or resourceful you are, there are limits to what one person can achieve. This is where the value of collaboration comes in. Successful partnerships bring together complementary skills, resources, and knowledge that you can't always achieve on your own.

The wealthiest individuals understand that collaboration is key to unlocking opportunities. A powerful partnership allows you to tap into new networks, access capital, gain expertise, and share risks—all while focusing on what each partner does best. The ability to **leverage other people's strengths** accelerates growth in ways that are nearly impossible to replicate alone.

Finding the Right Partners: Quality Over Quantity

Not all partnerships are created equal. While it might be tempting to partner with anyone who shares your vision, the most successful entrepreneurs know that **quality always trumps quantity**. The right partner is someone whose skills, values, and goals align with yours in a way that creates synergy.

When considering a partnership, look beyond the surface. Ask yourself:

- **Do they have complementary skills?** A great partnership works because both parties bring something unique to the table. Whether it's financial expertise, marketing prowess, or industry-specific knowledge, each partner should fill a gap that the other can't cover.

- **Do they share your values?** Shared values are the foundation of a strong partnership. Misalignment here can lead to misunderstandings, conflict, and ultimately the dissolution of the partnership. Make sure your potential partner has a similar vision for long-term success.

- **Can they contribute to your growth?** Great partners aren't just assets—they're catalysts. A good partner should challenge you, offer fresh perspectives, and help you reach new levels of success.

When you find the right fit, the partnership becomes a multiplier—expanding your reach, amplifying your efforts, and boosting your income.

The Role of Trust in Partnerships

Trust is the cornerstone of any successful partnership. Without trust, even the most promising collaborations will eventually break down. Wealthy entrepreneurs understand that building trust isn't something that happens overnight. It's earned through consistency, transparency, and shared experiences.

In a great partnership, both sides know they can rely on each other to follow through on commitments, be honest, and share in the rewards and risks. Trust allows for open communication and innovation, which can lead to game-changing ideas and strategies.

One of the best ways to build trust is to start small and see how the partnership unfolds. Don't rush into large-scale collaborations without taking time to understand the dynamics and how well you work together. Trust grows through action, so build a track record of mutual respect and reliability before moving on to more significant opportunities.

Leveraging Networks and Connections

Another key benefit of the right partnerships is the ability to tap into networks and connections. Often, success isn't just about what you know—it's about **who you know**. By aligning yourself with the right people, you open the door to new opportunities, relationships, and avenues for growth that you wouldn't have access to on your own.

Partners can introduce you to investors, mentors, customers, suppliers, or other potential collaborators who can help accelerate your growth. Networking through trusted partners often leads to high-quality connections that would be difficult to establish without the right relationships in place.

Risk Sharing: Protecting Yourself and Your Venture

When you're growing your wealth, taking risks is part of the game. But the wealthiest entrepreneurs understand that **smart risk-taking** involves minimizing personal exposure. Partnerships allow you to share the financial, operational, and emotional risks that come with scaling a business.

When you split the burden of risk, you're able to take bolder actions and explore new opportunities without putting everything on the line. With the right partner, you can take bigger swings—whether that means investing in a new project, entering a new market, or making a strategic acquisition—because the risk is more manageable when shared.

This shared responsibility ensures that if things don't go as planned, you have support in place to weather the storm. In contrast, solo ventures can sometimes be overwhelming and leave you vulnerable if challenges arise.

The Power of Expertise and Learning

One of the greatest accelerators of wealth is **learning from others**. The right partner can serve as a mentor, advisor, or teacher who helps you shortcut your path to success. This is particularly valuable when you're entering new industries, exploring unfamiliar markets, or developing new skills.

Partnering with someone who has already mastered a specific area of business can dramatically reduce your learning curve. Instead of trial and error, you get to bypass mistakes and adopt proven strategies. This is a major reason why ultra-wealthy individuals seek out mentors and industry leaders—they know that learning from others' experiences can save them time, money, and energy in the long run.

How to Make Partnerships Work for You

The best partnerships don't just happen—they're created through intentional effort, clear communication, and mutual respect. Here are a few tips for making partnerships work:

1. **Establish clear goals**: From the beginning, make sure both partners are aligned on the goals of the venture. Having a shared vision and understanding of each partner's role will help minimize misunderstandings later.

2. **Set expectations**: Be clear about what each partner will contribute, how profits will be shared, and how decisions will be made. Establishing these parameters upfront ensures smoother collaboration.

3. **Communicate regularly**: Strong communication is essential to a healthy partnership. Set regular meetings to check in, discuss challenges, and review progress. This will help keep both parties aligned and address issues before they escalate.

4. **Celebrate successes together**: Partnerships are about collaboration, not competition. Celebrate wins together and acknowledge the contributions of each partner. This fosters goodwill and ensures long-term success.

Conclusion: Multiply Your Success by Partnering Up

If you want to scale your wealth and income, **partnering with the right people** is one of the most powerful tools you have at your disposal. When you find individuals who complement your strengths, share your vision, and bring new resources and expertise to the table, the possibilities for growth are limitless.

Success isn't just about what you can achieve on your own—it's about building a network of people who can accelerate your progress, share risks, and help you reach new heights. So, look around. Who can you partner with to multiply your success and take your wealth to the next level? The right people will be your greatest asset on the road to extreme wealth.

Billionaire Wealth Stacking: Create Multiple Revenue Streams

One of the key strategies that separates the ultra-wealthy from the rest is their ability to create **multiple revenue streams**. Billionaires don't just rely on one source of income—they stack wealth by diversifying their earnings in ways that not only increase their overall wealth but also protect them from financial risks.

In this section, we'll explore how billionaires approach wealth stacking, why multiple revenue streams are essential, and how you can apply this strategy to your own life.

What Is Wealth Stacking?

Wealth stacking is a concept used by billionaires to describe the process of building and layering multiple sources of income. Instead of depending on one single venture, billionaires create income from various streams that complement and support each other. By doing this, they not only grow their wealth but also build financial resilience.

Think of it like building a house. Instead of just constructing one pillar to hold up the entire structure, billionaires build many pillars—each one strong and independent, but working together to support the whole. This diversification minimizes risk and maximizes potential returns.

Why Wealth Stacking Matters

1. **Risk Reduction**: By spreading your income sources across different industries or assets, you lower the risk of relying on a single stream that may fail. A business can go through tough times, but as long as you have other income streams in place, you won't be knocked out of the game.

2. **Exponential Growth**: Each new revenue stream has the potential to grow on its own, compounding the wealth you've already created. When done strategically, stacking wealth can result in exponential returns. For example, if you're earning money from both real estate and investments in tech startups, each of these areas can appreciate over time, multiplying your wealth without you needing to do much additional work.

3. **More Financial Freedom**: Having multiple streams of income provides greater financial stability. You're no longer tied to a single pay-check or one source of business. With the right stacking strategy, you can begin to create wealth even while you sleep, moving closer to true financial freedom.

4. **Leveraging Time**: Having multiple revenue streams allows you to leverage your time. While one business or investment may require attention, others might work on autopilot, generating income without constant oversight. This is crucial for scaling wealth efficiently.

How Billionaires Stack Wealth

Billionaires know that true wealth isn't just built through one big idea, it's built through **diversification**. Here's how they do it:

1. **Building Multiple Businesses**: Many billionaires don't just focus on one company. They create or invest in multiple businesses across different industries. For example, Jeff Bezos doesn't only run Amazon; he has investments in space exploration (Blue Origin), The Washington Post, and various tech ventures. By owning a portfolio of businesses, he can tap into various growth areas.

2. **Investing in Real Estate**: Real estate is a classic method for stacking wealth. Billionaires know that owning property provides steady cash flow, tax benefits, and long-term appreciation. By acquiring residential, commercial,

or even industrial properties, they ensure that their wealth is constantly growing from multiple angles—rents, asset appreciation, and tax advantages.

3. **Smart Stock Market Investments**: Billionaires use the stock market to generate passive income. They may own large stakes in companies, receiving dividends, or they may buy into startups with massive growth potential. Investment portfolios are a common feature in billionaire wealth stacking because the return can be substantial when you pick the right stocks or equity stakes.

4. **Intellectual Property and Licensing**: Many billionaires build wealth through intellectual property—such as patents, trademarks, or even popular content. They create or invest in intellectual property and then license it for profit. The tech industry is an excellent example, with companies like Apple, Microsoft, and Disney earning revenue from their patents, software, and franchises.

5. **Tech and Digital Assets**: In today's digital age, tech startups, cryptocurrencies, and digital assets offer rapid growth potential. Billionaires know how to spot emerging technologies and invest early in opportunities that can scale quickly. Whether it's developing a new app or investing in blockchain technology, digital assets have become a key part of wealth stacking for many wealthy individuals.

6. **Private Equity and Venture Capital**: Billionaires often get involved in venture capital or private equity, investing in small, high-potential startups. These investments often have the opportunity for huge returns, and even if one fails, the billionaires have diversified enough that they don't feel the impact. Plus, by being an early investor in a promising startup, they gain huge leverage when those companies grow and get acquired or go public.

How You Can Stack Your Own Wealth

The idea of stacking wealth might sound complex, but you can start with simple steps. Here's how to implement this strategy:

1. **Start with What You Know**: Begin by building wealth in areas that you're familiar with. Whether it's your business, a hobby you can turn into a side income, or a sector you understand well, starting with what you know will give you a solid foundation for scaling and diversification.

2. **Invest in Real Estate**: You don't have to be a billionaire to start investing in real estate. Look for properties that offer rental income or potential for appreciation. Real estate is one of the best ways to start stacking wealth because it's a tangible asset that can work for you over time.

3. **Look for Opportunities to Invest**: Start small with stocks, bonds, or mutual funds, and build a diversified portfolio. As your financial literacy grows, you can invest in more complex assets like startups or private equity.

4. **Create a Side Hustle**: Building a side hustle can be a great way to create additional streams of income. Whether it's freelance work, creating digital products, or starting an e-commerce business, a side hustle can eventually scale into a substantial revenue stream.

5. **Use Technology to Automate**: In the digital age, technology can be your best friend. Use it to create and automate income streams that require minimal effort to maintain. This could mean setting up an online course, writing a book, or creating a subscription-based service.

6. **Be Strategic with Your Time**: As you build your streams, focus on increasing efficiency. The most successful people don't spread themselves too thin. Instead, they figure out how to automate or delegate tasks so that they can focus on scaling their most profitable ventures.

Conclusion: The Power of Wealth Stacking

Billionaire wealth stacking isn't just about working harder—it's about working smarter and ensuring that your income comes from multiple reliable sources. By following the billionaire model of building and layering various income streams, you not only increase your wealth but also reduce your financial risk and enhance your opportunities for growth.

Start by focusing on one stream and then build from there. As you add more sources of income, you'll create a robust financial foundation that can withstand challenges, multiply your wealth, and provide you with the freedom to live on your terms. This is the power of wealth stacking—and it's a strategy anyone can use to build extreme wealth.

8

Managing and Protecting Your Wealth

The Wealthy Don't Save – They Invest

When it comes to building wealth, there's a fundamental mindset shift that separates the wealthy from everyone else. It's not about how much you save—it's about how much you invest. Saving money is often seen as the cornerstone of financial security, but for the wealthy, it's not enough. They understand that money is meant to grow, not just sit idle in a bank account.

This chapter will break down why the wealthy don't focus on saving, but rather on investing, and how you can apply this principle to your own financial journey.

The Illusion of Saving

Saving money is often encouraged because it feels safe. Put aside a percentage of your pay-check every month, and you'll build up a nest egg, right? While this approach works to some extent, it's far from the most effective strategy for creating wealth.

Here's the issue: when you save, you're essentially storing money that does not grow. At best, a savings account will give you a tiny interest rate, usually so low that it barely outpaces inflation. This means that the money you're saving today will be worth less tomorrow, leaving you with less purchasing power over time.

Saving can feel like a responsible financial decision, but it's a passive way of handling your money. It doesn't allow your wealth to compound or multiply. Instead, it keeps your money stagnant, which is exactly what the wealthy avoid at all costs.

The Power of Investing

Investing, on the other hand, is how the wealthy build their fortunes. When you invest, you put your money to work. Instead of it just sitting in a savings account, it's invested in assets that have the potential to grow—stocks, real estate, businesses, and more.

Billionaires know that their money should be working harder than they do. By investing, they're allowing their wealth to compound, increase in value, and generate more opportunities. Here's why this approach works so well:

1. **Compound Growth**: One of the most powerful forces in wealth creation is compounding. By investing your money, you can earn returns on your initial investment, and then those returns earn their own returns. Over time, this creates a snowball effect that leads to exponential growth. For example, a $10,000 investment that earns an average of 8% annually will grow to over $21,500 in 10 years—without you having to add a single penny.

2. **Asset Appreciation**: Investments, especially in real estate, stocks, or businesses, tend to increase in value over time. When you buy an asset, you're not just hoping to make some extra cash—you're betting on that asset's long-term appreciation. Real estate, for example, can increase in value due to factors like demand, location improvements, and inflation, turning your initial investment into a much larger sum.

3. **Multiple Streams of Income**: By investing, you create multiple streams of income that can provide financial security and independence. This is why the wealthy focus so heavily on investments. Through dividends from stocks, rental income from real estate, or profits from business ventures, the wealthy don't rely on one pay-check. They build an ecosystem of income that works for them, day and night.

4. **Leverage**: Wealthy investors also use leverage to multiply their wealth. Leverage means using borrowed money to increase the size of an investment, allowing them to control larger assets than they could afford with their own money. For example, when buying real estate, you might only need to put down a fraction of the total price, borrowing the rest. The goal is for the appreciation and income generated by the asset to more than cover

the debt. This way, you can make bigger investments and earn bigger returns, faster.

Why Saving Doesn't Cut It for the Wealthy

While saving is important for short-term emergencies or goals, it's not the strategy that the wealthy use to create true, long-lasting wealth. Here's why:

1. **Inflation**: The wealthier you get, the more you understand that inflation is your enemy. As the cost of living rises, the purchasing power of saved money decreases. To stay ahead of inflation, you need to invest your money in assets that will appreciate and grow faster than inflation.

2. **Risk and Reward**: Wealthy individuals understand that risk is part of the game. While there's always a risk when it comes to investing, there's also the potential for much higher rewards. Billionaires are willing to take calculated risks in exchange for bigger returns. Saving, however, doesn't involve risk— but it also doesn't offer the high rewards that investments do.

3. **Opportunity Cost**: By saving money in low-interest accounts, you miss out on opportunities to make your money work for you. Wealthy individuals see this as a huge missed opportunity. For example, rather than saving for years and waiting for a small return, they'll take that money and invest it in a business, real estate, or stocks, where it has the chance to grow exponentially.

4. **Creating Wealth**: The goal for the wealthy is not just to save, but to create. They want to create businesses, buy assets, and build opportunities that generate wealth over time. Saving doesn't create anything—it simply preserves. Investing, on the other hand, allows you to actively create wealth by owning and controlling valuable assets.

How You Can Start Investing Like the Wealthy

You don't need to be a billionaire to start investing. Here's how you can begin:

1. **Start Early**: The earlier you start investing, the more time your money has to grow. Begin by setting aside a portion of your income for investments, rather than savings. If you're unsure where to start, consider low-cost index

funds or exchange-traded funds (ETFs), which offer broad exposure to the market.

2. **Learn About Different Investment Options**: Stocks, bonds, mutual funds, real estate, and even business ownership all offer unique ways to invest. Educate yourself on these different investment options and choose the ones that align with your goals and risk tolerance.

3. **Focus on Long-Term Growth**: Investing isn't about quick wins. It's about patience and letting your money grow over time. Don't be tempted by get-rich-quick schemes—true wealth comes from consistent, long-term investment strategies.

4. **Diversify**: One of the smartest things you can do with your investments is to diversify. Don't put all your money into one type of asset. Spread it out over multiple investments—real estate, stocks, bonds, and more—to reduce risk and increase your chances of a high return.

5. **Consider Passive Investments**: If you're just getting started, look for passive investment opportunities that don't require a lot of active management. Real estate funds, dividend-paying stocks, and index funds are all ways to start building wealth without needing to constantly monitor your investments.

Conclusion: The Mindset Shift to Wealth

To build lasting wealth, you need to shift your mindset from a saver to an investor. Saving is important for stability, but it's investing that will truly grow your wealth and set you on the path to financial freedom. The wealthiest individuals in the world don't save—they invest. They put their money into assets that will multiply, and in doing so, they take advantage of the compounding power of wealth creation.

By learning to invest wisely, you can unlock the doors to wealth that saving alone will never open. So, stop thinking about saving and start thinking about investing—because that's the real path to building and protecting your wealth.

Tax Strategies of the Rich: Keeping More of What You Earn

One of the biggest secrets the wealthy use to protect and grow their wealth is smart tax planning. While many people dread tax season, the rich see it as an opportunity—a chance to legally minimize what they owe and keep more of their hard-earned money. This chapter will uncover the tax strategies that the rich use to protect their wealth and show you how you can apply these strategies to your own financial life.

The Power of Tax Planning

Most people treat taxes as something that just happens once a year. They file their returns, pay what they owe, and move on. But the wealthy understand that tax planning is an ongoing, year-round process that can make or break your financial future.

By actively managing their taxes, the rich ensure that they keep as much of their earnings as possible, allowing them to reinvest those savings into new opportunities. Taxes are not just a cost to be accepted—they're an expense that can be reduced through strategic planning.

The Difference Between Earning and Keeping Wealth

You can make all the money in the world, but if you don't have a strategy for keeping it, you won't be able to build lasting wealth. Taxes are one of the biggest barriers to wealth creation. For most people, taxes take a significant chunk of their income—often 30%, 40%, or even more, depending on where they live.

The wealthy, however, understand that the more you make, the more strategies you need to legally minimize those taxes. They don't just accept high tax rates—they actively work to reduce their tax burden through smart investment decisions, income splitting, deductions, and more.

How the Wealthy Minimize Taxes

Here are some of the key strategies the rich use to legally minimize their tax bills:

1. Income Splitting

One common strategy used by the wealthy is income splitting. This involves redistributing income between family members or legal entities (like trusts or corporations) to lower the overall family or business tax rate. For example, if one family member is in a lower tax bracket, income can be shifted to that person to take advantage of the lower rate.

This is a way to ensure that high-income earners don't pay as much in taxes by spreading income across multiple lower-tax individuals or entities.

2. Tax-Deferred Investments

Tax-deferred investments are another tool the wealthy use to grow their wealth without immediately paying taxes on the gains. Accounts like 401(k)s, IRAs, and other retirement plans allow money to grow without being taxed until it is withdrawn. The wealthy use these types of accounts to accumulate wealth without giving the government a cut until later.

In addition to retirement accounts, there are other tax-deferred investment strategies, such as using real estate depreciation. By owning property, you can deduct depreciation from your taxable income, lowering your taxes while still growing your wealth.

3. Capital Gains Tax Treatment

The wealthy understand the difference between earned income (like salaries or wages) and passive income (like capital gains from investments). Capital gains— the profits you make from selling assets like stocks, bonds, or real estate—are taxed at a much lower rate than regular income.

By focusing on investments that generate long-term capital gains, the wealthy minimize the amount they owe in taxes. Instead of earning money from a pay-check, which is taxed at the highest rates, they focus on investments that appreciate over time, paying taxes only when they sell the assets.

4. Utilizing Deductions and Credits

The wealthy know that there are many legal deductions and credits available that can reduce taxable income. These might include charitable contributions, business expenses, and investment-related costs. By structuring their finances in a way that maximizes these deductions, the rich reduce the amount they owe at tax time.

For example, the rich often donate to charities not only to give back but also to take advantage of tax deductions. By giving to causes they care about, they can lower their taxable income while supporting meaningful work in the world.

5. Real Estate and Depreciation

Real estate is a powerful tool for reducing taxes. The wealthy often invest in rental properties, which generate income but also provide tax benefits. One of the most significant advantages is depreciation—a legal tax deduction that allows property owners to deduct a portion of their property's value each year, even if the property is appreciating in the market.

This deduction can offset rental income and reduce overall tax liability. Even though the property's value may be increasing, the depreciation deduction means the property owner is paying less in taxes, making real estate one of the most effective tax-saving tools used by the wealthy.

6. Offshore Accounts and Tax Shelters

While controversial, some wealthy individuals use offshore accounts or tax shelters to minimize taxes legally. By setting up business entities or trusts in jurisdictions with lower tax rates, they can reduce their overall tax burden. This strategy requires careful legal planning, but for those who have the resources to navigate international tax laws, it can be an effective way to protect wealth.

Tax-Advantaged Accounts

Another simple yet powerful way the wealthy manage their taxes is by contributing to tax-advantaged accounts. These accounts are specifically designed to reduce the amount you owe by offering tax breaks, such as:

- **Retirement Accounts**: Accounts like 401(k)s or IRAs allow you to defer taxes on your contributions until you withdraw the money. This means you can save on taxes now and let your investments grow without being taxed in the meantime.

- **Health Savings Accounts (HSAs)**: These accounts allow you to save money for medical expenses without being taxed on your contributions, and the funds can grow tax-free.

By using tax-advantaged accounts, the wealthy grow their wealth with a tax shield, meaning more of their earnings are reinvested rather than taken by the government.

The Importance of Hiring Experts

While some of these strategies may seem complex, the wealthy often hire tax professionals—accountants, financial planners, and attorneys—to help them navigate the system. By working with experts, they ensure that they're taking full advantage of every available strategy while staying compliant with the law.

These professionals can provide valuable insight into structuring investments, setting up trusts, and ensuring that wealth is protected from excessive taxation. For anyone serious about wealth management, hiring the right experts is a key part of the equation.

Conclusion: Taking Control of Your Taxes

The rich don't just accept their tax bills—they take control of them. By using a combination of smart strategies like income splitting, tax-deferred investments, capital gains treatment, and real estate depreciation, they legally reduce their tax burden and keep more of their earnings.

While you may not have the same financial resources as a billionaire, you can start implementing these strategies right now. By learning the ins and outs of taxes and working with experts, you can reduce your tax liability, grow your wealth faster, and build a more secure financial future. The key is to think of taxes as a part of your financial plan, not just a burden to endure. When you take control, you'll be able to keep more of what you earn and use that money to build lasting wealth.

How Billionaires Legally Protect Their Wealth

When it comes to wealth, billionaires don't just focus on making money—they focus just as much on protecting it. Their wealth is their greatest asset, and they understand that protecting it is just as important as growing it. The rich know that without the right safeguards, wealth can slip away through taxes, lawsuits, or poor decisions.

But the best part? They don't rely on luck or guesswork. They use smart, legal strategies to ensure that their wealth stays secure, grows, and remains protected for generations. In this section, we'll explore the key strategies billionaires use to protect their wealth—and how you can apply some of these techniques to your own financial life.

1. Asset Protection through Trusts

One of the most common tools the wealthy use to protect their assets is a trust. A trust is a legal arrangement where you transfer ownership of your assets to a third party—the trustee—who manages them on behalf of the beneficiary.

Billionaires use different types of trusts to shield their wealth from creditors, lawsuits, or divorce settlements. A well-established trust can ensure that assets are passed on to heirs without going through probate, reducing taxes, and keeping wealth protected from claims.

For example, a **revocable trust** can be changed or cancelled at any time, giving the wealth holder flexibility. On the other hand, an **irrevocable trust** means that once assets are transferred, they are no longer considered part of the person's estate, making them immune to creditors and lawsuits.

Trusts also provide privacy, as they are not made public like a will, which means family members and beneficiaries can inherit wealth without it being widely known.

2. Limited Liability Companies (LLCs)

Another powerful tool the wealthy use for wealth protection is the creation of **Limited Liability Companies (LLCs)**. These are legal entities created to separate personal assets from business assets, providing liability protection. If the business is ever sued, only the company's assets are at risk, not the personal assets of the billionaire.

Billionaires often set up LLCs to own their real estate, investments, and other valuable assets. By doing so, they protect their personal wealth from being exposed to legal actions or business risks. Whether it's an investment property or a valuable art collection, LLCs are used to shield assets from creditors or lawsuits, ensuring their wealth remains intact.

3. Insurance: The Safety Net

Billionaires don't just rely on legal structures; they also use **insurance** as a way to protect themselves against unforeseen risks. Some billionaires invest in specialized insurance policies, such as **umbrella insurance**, which provides extra coverage beyond what normal insurance covers, or **asset protection insurance** that is specifically designed to protect wealth from lawsuits.

Life insurance policies are another tool in their wealth protection strategy. Many ultra-wealthy individuals use permanent life insurance to build up cash value over time, which can be borrowed against or used to offset taxes. By doing this, they can grow their wealth while having a backup plan to ensure their family is taken care of in case of the unexpected.

4. Diversification: Spreading the Risk

Another key principle billionaires use to protect their wealth is **diversification**. The wealthiest individuals know that concentrating too much in one area can be risky. That's why they spread their investments across multiple asset classes—stocks, real estate, private equity, commodities, art, and more.

By diversifying their wealth, billionaires reduce the risk of losing it all if one sector underperforms. If one area of their portfolio falters, other areas can still perform well and balance out any losses. This reduces the likelihood of significant financial damage and helps maintain long-term wealth.

5. International Assets and Offshore Accounts

Billionaires often take their wealth protection strategy one step further by **going international**. Offshore accounts and investments in foreign markets allow them to shield assets from domestic risks, such as higher taxes or economic instability.

Some billionaires use countries with more favorable tax laws to establish trusts, hold assets, or even set up businesses. Countries like Switzerland, the Cayman Islands, and Luxembourg have laws that protect wealth from excessive taxation or forced confiscation, providing an extra layer of security.

By holding a portion of their wealth offshore, billionaires can diversify their exposure to risk across different geopolitical climates. However, they do this with a clear understanding of the legal frameworks, ensuring everything is done within the bounds of the law.

6. Legacy Planning: Passing Wealth Without Penalties

Billionaires think long-term—not just about protecting their wealth today but also about protecting it for future generations. **Estate planning** is a critical part of this. The goal is to pass wealth on to heirs without triggering massive estate taxes, which can easily eat up a large portion of the estate.

Billionaires create **family foundations** or **charitable trusts** that allow them to pass wealth to their children or beneficiaries while minimizing taxes. By allocating wealth to a charitable cause, they can receive tax deductions while ensuring their legacy lives on. Not only does this protect their wealth, but it also allows them to make a lasting impact on the world.

Another estate planning tool they use is **generation-skipping trusts**, which allow wealth to be transferred to grandchildren or great-grandchildren, bypassing certain taxes that would apply if the wealth was passed directly to children.

7. Keeping Private: Financial Privacy

Many billionaires value their **financial privacy**. They go to great lengths to ensure that their wealth and financial dealings are kept private. This could involve using private investment firms, maintaining anonymous LLCs, and keeping low public profiles.

Billionaires understand that the more public your financial life is, the more exposed it becomes to potential risks—whether it's tax collectors, opportunistic lawsuits, or unwanted attention. Keeping their financial affairs private allows them to maintain control over their wealth while protecting it from public scrutiny.

8. Risk Management and Legal Counsel

Finally, billionaires surround themselves with a team of **trusted advisors**—including attorneys, accountants, and wealth managers—who specialize in wealth protection. These experts help them navigate complex legal landscapes, stay compliant with tax laws, and ensure their wealth is protected from any possible threat.

A top-tier legal team can provide invaluable advice on structuring businesses, handling estate matters, and identifying new opportunities for asset protection. Billionaires understand the importance of having experienced professionals on their side to handle the technicalities and protect their wealth in ways they might not even have considered.

Conclusion: Wealth Protection Is a Strategy, Not an Afterthought

The key takeaway from how billionaires protect their wealth is that wealth protection isn't just about luck or simply having a lot of money—it's a strategy. Billionaires put in the work to understand the legal, financial, and tax systems, then use that knowledge to their advantage.

By employing trusts, LLCs, insurance, diversification, and international investments, they reduce the risk of losing their wealth. And by surrounding themselves with experts and thinking long-term, they ensure that their wealth is not only protected but continues to grow for generations to come.

While these strategies may seem complex, you don't need to be a billionaire to use them. With the right knowledge and the right team, you can start implementing some of these strategies to protect and grow your own wealth. Remember, the rich don't just focus on making money—they focus just as much on protecting it. So should you.

Creating Long-Term Financial Security

In the world of business and investing, an **economic moat** is a term used to describe the competitive advantage that protects a company from its competitors. Just like a moat around a castle keeps invaders at bay, a strong economic moat safeguards your wealth from risks and uncertainties. For individuals aiming to build lasting financial security, creating your own personal economic moat is a powerful strategy.

But how do you build an economic moat around your wealth? The key is to establish a set of assets, systems, and strategies that not only generate income but also protect that income from outside threats. When you do this right, you create a solid foundation that provides stability, growth, and financial protection over the long term.

Let's break down how you can build and fortify your own economic moat.

1. Create Multiple Income Streams

One of the most effective ways to create a moat around your wealth is by developing **multiple streams of income**. Relying on a single source of income—like a pay-check from a job or a single business—puts you at risk if that income is interrupted.

Billionaires understand this concept well, which is why they diversify their earnings. Whether it's through investments in real estate, stocks, businesses, or passive income sources like royalties or dividends, creating different streams of income ensures that if one falls, the others can still support you.

For example, if you own rental properties, your rental income can help buffer you against stock market fluctuations. If you have investments in tech companies, those can continue to grow even when the economy goes through tough times. This diversification creates a cushion for you, making it harder for external challenges to disrupt your wealth.

2. Invest in Hard Assets

To build a moat that holds long-term value, **hard assets** like real estate, gold, or even valuable collectibles are key. Unlike stocks or bonds, hard assets tend to hold their value over time, even during market downturns.

Real estate, for instance, is a tried-and-true wealth builder because it appreciates in value over time and provides cash flow through rent. Gold and other precious metals are also great for diversifying and preserving wealth during inflation or financial crises. Hard assets serve as a foundation for your moat, providing both value and protection for your wealth.

This strategy helps insulate you from inflation, market crashes, and other economic upheavals. By owning physical assets, you build a buffer that allows your wealth to grow steadily, regardless of what's happening in the stock market or the global economy.

3. Develop Unique Skills or Intellectual Property

Another way to create a moat around your wealth is by **developing unique skills or intellectual property** that can't easily be copied. This could mean starting a business with a unique product or service, developing a brand with loyal customers, or even creating intellectual property like books, patents, or software.

The wealthy understand that their knowledge, expertise, and creativity are valuable. Once you have intellectual property that can generate royalties or licensing fees, you essentially create a recurring source of income that is unique to you. This is a moat that competitors can't easily breach because the skills or products are yours alone.

For example, creating a unique online course, a bestselling book, or an innovative tech solution gives you a sustainable edge over others. Even if others try to copy your work, your name, reputation, and experience make your product irreplaceable in the eyes of your audience.

4. Build Strong Relationships and Networks

Your relationships and network are a crucial part of your moat. Billionaires know that wealth is not just about money; it's about the people you know and how you work together. By forming strong connections with trusted advisors, business partners, mentors, and key players in your industry, you strengthen your financial position.

A network provides opportunities, insights, and safety nets. If you're facing a business challenge, your connections can help you navigate the situation. If you need capital, partners or investors from your network can step in to support you. Relationships also create opportunities for collaboration and partnership, allowing you to scale your wealth more rapidly.

Consider people who build a business empire by leveraging strategic partnerships. By aligning with others who bring complementary skills or resources to the table, you create a moat of opportunity and protection, one that insulates you from setbacks and opens doors to new ventures.

5. Protect Your Wealth with Legal Structures

An important aspect of building an economic moat is the legal structures you put in place to protect your assets. Trusts, LLCs (Limited Liability Companies), and other legal entities can help shield your wealth from taxes, lawsuits, and unforeseen events.

For instance, creating an LLC to hold real estate or business assets protects your personal wealth from being at risk in case of business debts or legal actions. Similarly, trusts can help shield wealth from excessive taxation or even safeguard it from being claimed in a lawsuit. This legal protection creates a barrier around your wealth, ensuring that no one can take it away from you easily.

6. Focus on Long-Term Thinking

Building an economic moat isn't about short-term gains or quick fixes—it's about **long-term security**. Billionaires think in terms of decades, not just months or years. They understand that wealth accumulation and protection require patience, discipline, and a long-term vision.

To create a moat that stands the test of time, you need to make decisions today that will pay off tomorrow. This means focusing on investments, assets, and strategies that will provide sustainable returns over time. Rather than chasing after fleeting trends, build wealth with steady, reliable sources that will continue to grow and provide you with stability in the future.

7. Constantly Reinforce and Adapt Your Moat

Finally, the process of building an economic moat is ongoing. Billionaires constantly refine their strategies, adapt to new opportunities, and make adjustments based on changing markets and conditions. They don't just build a moat and forget about it—they're always looking for ways to improve and reinforce it.

For you, this might mean staying educated about new investment opportunities, updating your legal protections, and diversifying your income streams even further. The world changes, and so should your approach to wealth building.

Reinforcing your moat ensures that it remains strong and resilient in the face of challenges.

Conclusion: Your Moat, Your Fortress

Creating a personal economic moat is about more than just making money—it's about **protecting** it, growing it, and ensuring it can withstand whatever the world throws at you. By developing multiple income streams, investing in hard assets, leveraging unique skills, and putting legal protections in place, you can build a fortress around your wealth.

The process takes time and strategy, but the rewards are worth it. Just like a well-constructed moat protects a castle from invaders, your economic moat will provide you with long-term financial security, allowing your wealth to grow and thrive in an ever-changing world.

So, start today—take small, consistent steps to build your moat. The stronger it becomes, the more impenetrable your wealth will be. And soon, you'll have a financial foundation that not only supports you but also ensures lasting success for generations to come.

9

Thriving in Uncertain Times

How the Ultra-Rich Prepare for Economic Downturns

While most people fear economic downturns, the ultra-rich view them as opportunities rather than threats. They don't panic or make rash decisions when the market drops. Instead, they have a strategic mindset that helps them not only survive but thrive during uncertain times. So, how do they prepare for economic downturns? Let's take a closer look.

1. Diversifying Investments to Minimize Risk

One of the most powerful strategies the ultra-rich use to prepare for downturns is **diversifying their investments**. Instead of putting all their money in one place—such as stocks or a single business—they spread it across different sectors and asset types. This includes a mix of:

- **Real estate:** Properties often hold their value, even during economic crises, and can generate consistent rental income.

- **Bonds:** Safe, stable investments that offer returns even when other markets are volatile.

- **Precious metals:** Gold and silver have historically been safe havens in times of economic uncertainty.

- **Private equity and businesses:** These investments can provide high returns, especially if they are in industries that can withstand economic turbulence.

By spreading their wealth across various assets, the ultra-rich minimize the risk of losing everything in one market crash. Even if one part of the economy takes a hit, other investments can continue to grow or provide stability.

2. Building Liquidity for Flexibility

The ultra-rich understand that in times of crisis, cash is king. While they still make smart investments, they also make sure to have substantial **liquidity**—money that is easily accessible in case of an emergency or a unique opportunity.

This could mean holding a portion of wealth in cash or cash-equivalents like money market accounts or short-term bonds. When markets are in turmoil, having liquidity allows the ultra-rich to take advantage of opportunities that others may miss, such as buying distressed assets at a discount or investing in undervalued stocks.

Being liquid doesn't mean being reckless with cash. The ultra-rich know how to balance their wealth, making sure their assets are well-positioned to grow while keeping enough liquidity to act when the time is right.

3. Investing in Businesses that Thrive During Crises

The ultra-rich are always thinking ahead and tend to invest in industries or businesses that are **recession-resistant**. These are companies that continue to perform well even when times are tough.

Some of these industries include:

- **Healthcare and pharmaceuticals:** People still need medical care, and healthcare companies often thrive during downturns.

- **Technology and innovation:** As the world becomes more tech-driven, companies in this space continue to grow, even when the economy is shaky.

- **Consumer staples:** Products people use every day—such as food, cleaning supplies, and hygiene products—remain in demand no matter the economic climate.

- **Utilities:** Electricity, water, and gas are essential services that people need, even during tough times.

By investing in these types of industries, the ultra-rich make sure their wealth continues to grow, even during recessions.

4. Hedging Against Inflation and Market Volatility

To protect their wealth, the ultra-rich often use **hedging strategies** that safeguard their assets against inflation and market fluctuations. A common strategy is to invest in **commodities** like gold, silver, or oil, which tend to perform well when inflation rises.

Another approach is through **hedge funds** or private equity firms that specialize in risk management. These funds can employ various strategies, including short selling, options trading, or buying assets that perform well in a volatile market. The goal is to offset any potential losses in other areas of their portfolio by using investments that thrive during uncertain times.

5. Staying Debt-Free or Minimizing Debt Exposure

While many people rely heavily on loans and credit during an economic downturn, the ultra-rich know the dangers of being over-leveraged. **Minimizing debt** is crucial to weathering financial storms.

During times of economic instability, high levels of debt can become a huge burden, as interest rates rise and income streams fluctuate. The ultra-rich avoid accumulating too much debt and focus on paying down existing obligations before taking on new risks. When the economy contracts, they have the financial flexibility to navigate through downturns without the weight of excessive borrowing.

6. Building a Strong Network for Strategic Advice

The ultra-rich understand the value of **networking**—but not just any network. They surround themselves with a team of trusted advisors: financial planners, lawyers, accountants, and even mentors who have successfully navigated economic downturns in the past.

During challenging times, they rely on this team to help them make informed decisions about their investments, tax strategies, and business operations. Their advisors provide insight into emerging opportunities or risks, helping them stay ahead of the curve and make smarter choices.

7. Focusing on Long-Term Goals

While many people panic during recessions and sell off investments at a loss, the ultra-rich stay focused on **long-term wealth creation**. They know that downturns are part of the natural market cycle and often present opportunities for those with patience and vision.

By maintaining a long-term mindset, the ultra-rich avoid making knee-jerk reactions that could harm their financial future. They don't let short-term market volatility distract them from their bigger goals, and they continue to invest with a view toward growth over decades, not just quarters.

8. Learning from Past Crises

Finally, the ultra-rich have a **learning mindset**. They understand that every downturn is an opportunity to grow wiser. After each economic crash, they analyze what worked, what didn't, and how they can adapt their strategy for the next downturn.

This ability to reflect and adjust is crucial to their success. Instead of viewing economic uncertainty as something to fear, they see it as a chance to fine-tune their approach and be better prepared for the future.

Conclusion: Thriving Through Preparedness

The ultra-rich don't wait until the storm hits—they prepare in advance. Through diversification, liquidity, smart business investments, hedging strategies, and a long-term focus, they protect and grow their wealth even in the most uncertain times.

If you want to thrive during economic downturns, follow their lead. Build a financial plan that accounts for volatility, create resilience through diversified investments, and develop the mindset to see opportunities where others see fear. By doing so, you can transform uncertain times into a stepping stone for even greater wealth.

The Billionaire Recession Playbook: Buying Assets When Others Panic

When the economy takes a downturn, most people panic. They rush to sell their stocks, hoard cash, and brace for the worst. But billionaires? They see opportunity. Instead of retreating, they go on a buying spree. They scoop up valuable assets at a discount, setting themselves up for even greater wealth when the market recovers. This is how the ultra-rich play the game—and if you understand their strategy, you can do the same.

1. The Mindset of a Contrarian Investor

The average investor follows the crowd. When the market is booming, they buy in at high prices. When fear takes over and prices plummet, they sell at a loss. Billionaires, on the other hand, do the opposite. They understand that **fear creates opportunity**. They know that downturns are temporary and that the biggest fortunes are built during times of uncertainty.

One of the greatest investors of all time, Warren Buffett, summed it up perfectly: *"Be fearful when others are greedy, and greedy when others are fearful."*

When the masses panic, billionaires see a golden opportunity to buy high-quality assets at bargain prices.

2. Why Recessions Create the Best Buying Opportunities

During a recession, fear takes over. People lose confidence in the economy, businesses struggle, and investors rush to sell their holdings. As a result, stock prices, real estate values, and even entire businesses can drop **far below their actual worth**.

For those with the **cash and courage** to invest, this is the perfect time to buy. Think of it like a clearance sale—except instead of getting discounts on clothes or gadgets, you're getting once-in-a-lifetime deals on assets that can generate wealth for decades.

Some of the best-performing investments in history were made **during market crashes**. Billionaires understand this, and that's why they **don't just survive recessions—they profit from them**.

3. What Billionaires Buy When Others Panic

So, what do billionaires invest in during recessions? Here are the key assets they target:

A. Stocks of Great Companies

When the stock market crashes, most investors panic-sell, even if the underlying companies are strong. Billionaires take advantage of this by **buying shares of blue-chip companies at a discount**.

They look for businesses that:

- Have a **proven track record** of profitability

- Are **leaders in their industry**

- Have strong **cash flow and low debt**

Tech giants, consumer goods companies, and essential service providers often survive recessions and come out stronger. The key is to **buy quality businesses when they're temporarily undervalued**.

B. Real Estate at Bargain Prices

Economic downturns often lead to declining real estate prices, especially in commercial and high-end residential markets. Billionaires capitalize on this by **buying premium properties at a discount**.

They look for:

- **Undervalued properties** in prime locations

- **Distressed sellers** who need quick cash

- **Income-generating assets** like rental properties

Real estate is one of the safest wealth-building tools, and buying when prices are low can lead to **massive gains when the market rebounds**.

C. Undervalued Businesses

During a recession, many small and mid-sized businesses struggle to stay afloat. Some of them have great potential but are under financial pressure. Billionaires and private equity firms **acquire these businesses at a fraction of their true value**, restructure them, and sell them later for a fortune.

Companies in sectors like healthcare, technology, and essential goods tend to be **resilient** during downturns and can be great long-term investments.

D. Alternative Assets (Gold, Bitcoin, Art, and More)

Billionaires also invest in **alternative assets** that hold their value during economic downturns. This can include:

- **Gold and silver**, which tend to rise when stock markets crash

- **Bitcoin and cryptocurrencies**, which some view as "digital gold"

- **Fine art and collectibles**, which can appreciate over time

These assets help **protect wealth** while other markets are in turmoil.

4. The Power of Cash Reserves: Being Ready to Strike

One reason billionaires can take advantage of downturns is that they **always have cash on hand**. They don't tie up all their money in investments—they keep a portion liquid, waiting for the right moment to **deploy capital when prices drop**.

This is why **having an emergency fund or an opportunity fund** is crucial for anyone who wants to profit during downturns. Even a small amount of cash, if invested wisely during a market dip, can turn into a **huge return when the economy recovers**.

5. The Patience Game: Thinking Long-Term

The secret to wealth-building during a recession isn't just **buying at the right time—it's holding on until the market recovers**.

Billionaires don't expect instant results. They buy when prices are low, wait for the economy to recover, and **sell when their assets have appreciated significantly**. This can take years, but the returns can be **life-changing**.

For example, during the 2008 financial crisis, stocks of major companies like Amazon, Apple, and Netflix plummeted. Investors who **had the courage to buy and hold** saw their investments **multiply tenfold** over the next decade.

6. You Don't Need to Be a Billionaire to Use This Strategy

You might be thinking: *"I don't have billions to invest—how can I apply this strategy?"* The truth is, **you don't need to be a billionaire to take advantage of market downturns**. You just need the right mindset and approach.

- **Start small:** Even a few hundred or thousand dollars invested wisely during a downturn can grow significantly over time.

- **Educate yourself:** Study market trends, learn how to evaluate assets, and seek expert advice.

- **Be patient:** Don't try to time the market perfectly. Focus on buying quality assets and holding them for the long run.

Final Thoughts: Recessions Create Millionaires—If You're Prepared

The difference between those who struggle during a recession and those who **build generational wealth** comes down to mindset and preparation. The ultra-rich **don't fear recessions—they prepare for them**. They **keep cash reserves, look for undervalued opportunities, and invest with a long-term perspective**.

Instead of seeing downturns as financial disasters, start viewing them as **rare wealth-building opportunities**. When others panic, **stay calm, do your research, and invest wisely**. Because history has shown us that **the biggest fortunes are built when the market is at its lowest**.

Building Resilient Wealth Through Diversification

The average person depends on a single income stream—usually a job. If that pay-check stops, financial disaster follows. The wealthy, on the other hand, have **multiple income streams**. Even if one dries up, the others keep flowing, keeping them financially secure no matter what happens.

Diversification works because **different types of assets and income sources perform differently under various market conditions**. When stocks go down, real estate may still appreciate. When businesses struggle, commodities like gold might rise in value.

How to Diversify Like the Wealthy

The wealthy don't just buy random investments—they **strategically spread their money across different asset classes**. Here's how you can do the same:

1. Stocks and Equities: Owning a Piece of Growing Companies

Stocks are one of the best ways to build wealth over time. But smart investors **don't just buy a handful of stocks in one industry**—they spread their investments across:

- **Blue-chip stocks** (large, stable companies like Apple, Microsoft, and Coca-Cola)

- **Growth stocks** (emerging businesses with high potential, like tech startups)

- **Dividend stocks** (companies that pay consistent cash returns)

- **Index funds and ETFs** (bundles of stocks that provide automatic diversification)

By investing in different sectors—technology, healthcare, finance, and consumer goods—you protect yourself from losing everything if one industry crashes.

2. Real Estate: Owning Income-Producing Assets

The rich **love real estate** because it generates passive income and appreciates over time. But they don't just buy one type of property—they diversify within real estate too:

- **Rental properties** (apartments, houses, or commercial buildings that provide steady cash flow)

- **REITs (Real Estate Investment Trusts)** (hands-free real estate investments that pay dividends)

- **Vacation rentals** (short-term rentals in high-demand tourist areas)

- **Land investments** (undeveloped land that can appreciate in value)

By owning different types of real estate in different locations, you **minimize risk and maximize returns**.

3. Businesses and Private Equity: Owning and Investing in Companies

Billionaires don't just **invest in businesses—they own them**. And they don't rely on just one venture; they build **multiple revenue streams** through:

- **Starting businesses** in different industries

- **Investing in private companies** with strong growth potential

- **Partnering with other entrepreneurs** to expand their reach

Having ownership in different types of businesses ensures that if one sector slows down, the others keep growing.

4. Commodities and Alternative Investments: Protecting Against Market Fluctuations

When stock markets crash, alternative assets **hold their value**. That's why the wealthy invest in:

- **Gold and silver** (hedges against inflation and economic crises)

- **Cryptocurrency** (digital assets like Bitcoin that provide diversification)

- **Fine art and collectibles** (rare items that appreciate over time)

- **Farmland and agricultural investments** (essential industries that remain stable)

These assets act as a financial cushion during economic downturns.

5. Cash and Liquidity: Always Being Ready to Strike

Billionaires **always keep cash on hand**—not because they're afraid, but because they want to be **ready to invest when opportunities arise**. During recessions, when assets are at rock-bottom prices, those with cash can **buy at a discount and build massive wealth**.

Keeping part of your portfolio in cash, high-yield savings accounts, or low-risk bonds ensures you have liquidity for future investments.

The Secret to Long-Term Financial Stability: Balance and Adaptability

Diversification isn't about **chasing every new investment trend**—it's about **balancing risk and reward**. The goal is to have a mix of **growth-oriented assets (stocks, businesses) and stability-focused assets (real estate, gold, cash reserves)**.

And most importantly, diversification isn't **set in stone**. The wealthy constantly **re-evaluate and adjust their investments** based on market trends, economic conditions, and new opportunities.

Final Thoughts: Build Wealth That Can Withstand Any Storm

If you want to build lasting wealth, **never rely on just one income stream or investment type**. Spread your wealth across different assets, industries, and markets. This way, no single crisis can take you down.

Diversification is the foundation of **financial resilience**. It's the reason billionaires don't panic during recessions—they know their wealth is spread across multiple **strong, income-generating assets**.

Start diversifying today. The more streams of income and investments you build, the stronger your financial future will be.

The Secret to Staying ahead of Financial Trends

Wealth isn't just about what you earn—it's about what you know **before everyone else knows it**. The ultra-rich don't wait for opportunities to come to them; they **see trends before they happen** and position themselves to profit. Staying ahead of financial trends is a superpower that can help you build and protect your wealth, even in uncertain times.

So how do billionaires and top investors predict where the money is flowing next? They follow a **simple but powerful strategy**:

1. Follow the Smart Money

The wealthiest people don't take random risks—they make **calculated moves** based on where other successful investors are putting their money. They study the actions of:

- Billionaires like Warren Buffett and Jeff Bezos

- Major investment firms like BlackRock and Vanguard

- Government policies that hint at future economic shifts

When you see where **big money** is flowing, you can ride the same wave instead of fighting against it.

How to Apply This:

- Read financial reports and investor letters from top billionaires.

- Track where venture capitalists and private equity firms are investing.

- Pay attention to government spending plans—where money is being allocated often signals the next big industry boom.

2. Stay on Top of Emerging Industries

Every decade, new industries emerge that create **massive wealth** for those who get in early. Think about how people who invested in **tech in the 1990s, crypto in the early 2010s**, or **electric vehicles before they became mainstream** made fortunes.

Industries with huge future potential include:

- **Artificial Intelligence (AI)** – Revolutionizing business, automation, and daily life.

- **Renewable Energy** – Governments worldwide are pushing for cleaner solutions.

- **Space Exploration & Travel** – Companies like SpaceX and Blue Origin are opening new frontiers.

- **Biotechnology & Longevity** – The business of extending human life is worth trillions.

- **Blockchain & Decentralized Finance (DeFi)** – Changing how we handle money and transactions.

How to Apply This:

- Follow tech leaders and futurists (Elon Musk, Cathie Wood, etc.).

- Read industry reports and trend forecasts.

- Invest small amounts early in companies leading new trends.

3. Leverage Data—Not Just Opinions

Most people make financial decisions based on **gut feelings, the news, or what their friends say**. The wealthy, on the other hand, use **data and research** to make smarter choices.

How to Apply This:

- Use financial tools like **Google Trends, stock screeners, and economic reports** to see patterns.

- Follow **macro trends**, such as interest rates, inflation, and employment data.

- Study historical cycles—markets tend to repeat themselves in predictable ways.

4. Build a Network of High-Level Thinkers

One of the biggest secrets of the ultra-wealthy is that they **don't operate alone**. They surround themselves with people who have **insider knowledge, connections, and expertise**.

Your network is your **shortcut to new financial opportunities**.

How to Apply This:

- Join investment groups, mastermind communities, and high-level networking events.

- Follow and engage with thought leaders in finance, tech, and business.

- Get a mentor—someone who has already built the wealth you aspire to.

5. Be Adaptable—Don't Cling to the Past

The biggest financial mistakes happen when people **refuse to change**. Industries rise and fall. What worked 20 years ago **won't always work today**. The rich understand this and **pivot quickly** when new opportunities arise.

Think about:

- Blockbuster refusing to adapt to streaming—Netflix took over.

- Taxi companies ignoring ride-sharing—Uber changed the game.

- Retailers ignoring e-commerce—Amazon dominated them.

The lesson? **Stay flexible. Be willing to evolve with new trends.**

Final Thoughts: Predict the Future, Profit from It

Staying ahead of financial trends isn't about guessing—it's about **paying attention to the right signals**. Follow the money, study emerging industries, leverage data, build a powerful network, and stay adaptable.

The future belongs to those who **see opportunities before the rest of the world does**. If you start thinking like the ultra-rich, you won't just survive uncertain times—you'll **thrive**.

10

Billionaire Habits & Daily Routines

Daily mindset & Productivity Habits of the Ultra-Wealthy

Success isn't an accident—it's a **habit**. The ultra-wealthy don't wake up and hope for a good day. They **design** their days for maximum productivity, focus, and success. If you want to reach extreme wealth, you need to think and operate like those who have already made it.

Here's a breakdown of the **daily habits and mindset** that billionaires use to stay ahead:

1. They Start the Day with Purpose

Wealthy people don't roll out of bed and scroll through social media. They begin their mornings with **intention**—a structured routine that sets the tone for success.

Common billionaire morning habits:

- **Wake up early** (usually before 6 AM) to get a head start.

- **Exercise** to boost energy and mental clarity.

- **Meditation or visualization** to focus on big goals.

- **Journaling or gratitude practice** to maintain a positive mindset.

How to Apply This:

- Wake up one hour earlier than usual and use that time for self-improvement.

- Try meditation or journaling to clear your mind before the day begins.

- Get your body moving—exercise isn't just for health; it sharpens your focus.

2. They Prioritize High-Impact Work

Billionaires don't waste time on distractions. They focus on **what moves the needle**—tasks that bring the biggest results.

They use a simple rule: **Do the hardest, most important task first.**

This is called **"Eating the Frog"**—a term made famous by productivity experts. If you tackle the biggest challenge early in the day, everything else feels easier.

How to Apply This:

- Identify **one high-impact task** every morning and get it done first.

- Avoid email and social media in the first hour of work—it kills focus.

- Work in **deep focus blocks** (90-minute sprints) to maximize productivity.

3. They Guard Their Time Like a Billion-Dollar Asset

The rich know that **time is their most valuable resource**. They don't let others steal it with unnecessary meetings, distractions, or small tasks that don't matter.

Instead, they:

- **Say no** to anything that doesn't align with their big goals.

- **Outsource and delegate** low-value tasks to free up time.

- **Use calendars religiously**—every minute is scheduled with purpose.

How to Apply This:

- Audit your day—what tasks are **stealing your time**? Eliminate or delegate them.

- Set strict boundaries for meetings and emails.

- Use a **calendar system** to schedule your entire day.

4. They Continuously Learn & Adapt

Billionaires are **obsessed** with learning. They know that **knowledge compounds**, just like money.

Most top CEOs read **one book per week**. Warren Buffett, for example, spends **80% of his day reading**. Elon Musk taught himself rocket science by reading books.

But it's not just about reading—it's about **learning from experience and adapting quickly**.

How to Apply This:

- Read **at least 30 minutes a day**—choose books on business, investing, or personal growth.

- Surround yourself with **mentors and successful people** who can challenge your thinking.

- Be willing to **change and pivot**—what worked yesterday might not work tomorrow.

5. They Take Care of Their Health & Energy

You can't build extreme wealth if you're always exhausted. The ultra-wealthy treat their bodies like high-performance machines.

They focus on:

- **Quality sleep** (at least 6–8 hours per night) to recharge.

- **Healthy eating**—fueling the body with the right foods.

- **Stress management**—through meditation, exercise, or hobbies.

They know that when their **body and mind are strong, their decisions and performance improve**.

How to Apply This:

- Get **consistent sleep**—avoid late-night screens and caffeine before bed.

- Eat **brain-boosting foods**—nuts, fish, leafy greens, and lean proteins.

- Make exercise a **non-negotiable part of your routine**.

6. They Stay Laser-Focused on Their Goals

The ultra-wealthy don't let **short-term distractions** pull them off course. They think **long-term** and stay committed to their vision.

Every day, they:

- **Review their goals** to stay aligned with their bigger purpose.

- **Measure progress**—tracking numbers and results to stay accountable.

- **Stay adaptable**—if something isn't working, they adjust quickly.

How to Apply This:

- Set clear financial and business goals and review them every morning.

- Track your daily progress—what's working, what needs improvement?

- Stay committed to your vision, even when obstacles arise.

Final Thoughts: Success Is a System, Not Luck

Wealth isn't about luck—it's about having a **daily system that guarantees success**. The ultra-wealthy follow a routine that maximizes their productivity, energy, and focus every single day.

If you want to join them, start adopting these habits now. **Design your day like a billionaire, and you'll start seeing billionaire-level results.**

The Role of Health, Fitness and Mental Clarity in Wealth Creation

Wealth isn't just about money. True wealth means having the energy, mental sharpness, and physical strength to enjoy success and keep building it. The ultra-wealthy understand a simple truth: **if your body and mind aren't in peak condition, your wealth will suffer.**

Think about it—what good is financial success if you're too exhausted, sick, or stressed to enjoy it? That's why the world's top performers make health, fitness, and mental clarity a **non-negotiable** part of their daily routines.

1. Energy is the Foundation of Success

Wealth requires **long-term thinking, smart decision-making, and relentless execution**—all of which demand high energy levels. The richest people in the world don't drag themselves through the day fueled by caffeine and stress. They optimize their bodies for **sustained energy and peak performance**.

How they do it:

- **Daily exercise** – It's not about bodybuilding or running marathons; it's about movement that keeps the body strong and the mind sharp. Many billionaires swear by morning workouts because they boost productivity and mental focus.

- **Hydration & nutrition** – They avoid junk food that drains energy and instead fuel their bodies with high-quality proteins, healthy fats, and nutrient-dense foods.

- **Sleep discipline** – They treat sleep as an investment, not an afterthought. Proper rest enhances decision-making, creativity, and emotional resilience.

How to apply this:

- Schedule at least **30 minutes of movement daily**—walk, lift weights, or do yoga.

- Drink more water and **cut out processed foods**—fuel your body like a high-performance engine.

- Create a **consistent sleep routine**—aim for 6–8 hours of high-quality rest.

2. Mental Clarity: The Hidden Key to Wealth

A **foggy mind leads to poor decisions.** In business and investing, one bad decision can cost millions. That's why billionaires prioritize **mental clarity**—they train their minds like athletes train their bodies.

How they do it:

- **Meditation & mindfulness** – Jeff Bezos, Ray Dalio, and other billionaires practice daily meditation to improve focus and reduce stress.

- **Digital detox** – They don't let endless notifications and social media distractions hijack their mental energy.

- **Strategic breaks** – Many top CEOs work in deep-focus sprints, followed by intentional downtime to recharge.

How to apply this:

- Start with **5 minutes of meditation daily**—it's proven to improve focus and reduce stress.

- Turn off **non-essential notifications** and reclaim your attention.

- Take **mental breaks**—even short walks can help you reset and refocus.

3. Stress Management: The Billionaire's Secret Weapon

High achievers face **massive pressure**, but they don't let stress control them. Instead, they build resilience by **managing stress proactively**.

How they do it:

- **They reframe challenges** – Instead of seeing problems as threats, they view them as opportunities to grow.

- **They surround themselves with the right people** – A strong network helps them handle challenges with perspective and support.

- **They invest in recovery** – Massages, cold therapy, and time in nature aren't luxuries; they're tools to reset and refocus.

How to apply this:

- When stress hits, **ask yourself: What's the opportunity here?**

- Build a **strong support system**—mentors, coaches, and like-minded peers.

- Prioritize recovery—spend time in nature, get massages, or try breathing exercises.

Final Thoughts: Your Body & Mind Are Your Greatest Assets

Money means nothing if you don't have the health to enjoy it. The ultra-wealthy don't treat health as a luxury—they treat it as **a critical investment in their success.**

If you want to build and sustain wealth, **start by taking care of your body and mind.** Energy, focus, and mental clarity will give you the edge you need to create, scale, and protect your wealth for the long haul.

How the Rich Learn Faster and Adapt to Change

The world's wealthiest people have one superpower that separates them from everyone else: **they learn fast and adapt even faster.** In today's rapidly changing world, the ability to absorb new information, unlearn outdated ideas, and pivot when necessary is what keeps them ahead. While most people resist change, the ultra-rich embrace it—and that's why they keep winning.

1. They Have a Growth Mindset

Successful people don't see intelligence or skill as fixed traits. They believe **everything can be learned, improved, and mastered.** Whether it's investing, technology, or leadership, they approach every challenge with curiosity and a willingness to grow.

How they do it:

- They ask **"What can I learn from this?"** instead of saying, "I don't know how to do that."

- They **seek feedback** and are willing to change their approach.

- They don't fear failure—they see it as **a lesson, not a loss.**

How to apply this:

- The next time you face a challenge, **ask yourself what you can learn from it.**

- Replace the phrase **"I can't"** with **"I haven't learned how yet."**

- Treat failure as feedback—adjust, improve, and try again.

2. They Read, Listen, and Learn Every Day

Warren Buffett, Bill Gates, and Elon Musk have one habit in common: **they never stop learning.** Buffett reads for hours each day, Gates takes "reading vacations," and Musk taught himself rocket science by devouring books.

How they do it:

- They **read books, listen to audiobooks, and follow experts** in their field.

- They **surround themselves with people who challenge their thinking.**

- They **invest in courses, coaching, and mentorship** to speed up their learning.

How to apply this:

- Read **at least 10 pages a day** of a book that expands your thinking.

- Listen to **podcasts and audiobooks** while commuting or exercising.

- Find a **mentor or coach** who can guide you faster than trial and error.

3. They Stay Ahead of Trends

The ultra-wealthy don't wait for change to happen—they **see it coming and prepare.** They invest in industries before they boom, adopt new technologies before the masses, and shift strategies before crises hit.

How they do it:

- They follow **cutting-edge research, industry reports, and global trends.**

- They **network with top thinkers** and innovators.

- They experiment with new ideas and **aren't afraid to pivot.**

How to apply this:

- Stay informed—**follow industry news, read reports, and watch global trends.**

- Network with people who are **smarter, faster, and more experienced than you.**

- Be flexible—if the world shifts, **adjust your strategy instead of resisting change.**

4. They Take Action—Fast

Learning is useless without action. The rich don't just consume knowledge—they apply it immediately. While most people wait until they feel "ready," the wealthy know that **action creates clarity, not the other way around.**

How they do it:

- They **test ideas quickly** instead of overthinking.

- They make **calculated risks** and learn from the results.

- They refine and improve along the way.

How to apply this:

- Stop waiting for the "perfect time"—**start now and adjust as you go.**

- Take small, calculated risks—**experience is the best teacher.**

- Track what works and what doesn't—**double down on success, pivot from failure.**

Final Thoughts: Learn Fast, Adapt Faster

The rich get richer because they **outlearn and out-adapt** everyone else. They aren't afraid of change—they use it as fuel for success. If you want to build wealth, make learning a daily habit and be willing to evolve. **The faster you learn and adapt, the faster you grow your wealth.**

The 10-Year Billionaire Roadmap: A step-by-Step Action Plan

Building massive wealth isn't about luck—it's about strategy, discipline, and playing the long game. The ultra-rich don't just dream of success; they follow a roadmap that takes them from where they are to where they want to be. If you want to create generational wealth, here's a **10-year blueprint** to get you there.

Year 1: Build a Wealth Mindset & Financial Discipline

Before you make millions (or billions), you need to think like the ultra-wealthy. Most people stay broke because they **fear risk, avoid learning, and spend instead of investing.**

Your action plan:

☑ Read at least **one finance, investing, or business book per month**

☑ Cut unnecessary expenses and start **automating your savings & investments**

☑ Build a **six-month emergency fund** to remove financial stress

☑ Start networking with people **who are wealthier and smarter than you**

Years 2-3: Increase Your Income & Build Multiple Revenue Streams

You can't save your way to wealth—you need **big money coming in.** Now's the time to maximize your earning potential.

Your action plan:

☑ Get **high-income skills** (sales, investing, coding, digital marketing, AI, etc.)

☑ Start a **side business, freelancing, or investing in cash-flowing assets**

☑ Focus on **scaling your main income source** (business, job, or investments)

☑ Invest at least **20-50% of your income** into assets that grow over time

Years 4-5: Master Investing & Build Passive Income

Now that your income is growing, your goal is to **make your money work for you.** Investing isn't optional—it's the only way to create lasting wealth.

Your action plan:

☑ Invest in **stocks, real estate, businesses, or other cash-flowing assets**

☑ **Diversify your investments** so you're not reliant on one income source

☑ Learn the **tax loopholes of the wealthy** to legally keep more of your earnings

☑ Start automating your **passive income streams** (rental properties, dividends, royalties, digital assets, etc.)

Years 6-7: Scale Your Business, Brand & Network

At this stage, you should have solid income streams and growing investments. Now, it's time to **10x your wealth by scaling what works.**

Your action plan:

☑ If you have a business, **automate, delegate, and expand it globally**

☑ If you're investing, **go bigger—acquire real estate, buy businesses, or fund startups**

☑ Build a **powerful network of high-net-worth individuals & industry leaders**

☑ Protect your wealth by setting up **trusts, LLCs, and tax-efficient strategies**

Years 8-9: Play at the Billionaire Level

The ultra-rich don't just build businesses—they own **systems, industries, and market influence.** Now is the time to think even bigger.

Your action plan:

☑ Invest in **massive wealth multipliers** (private equity, venture capital, large-scale real estate)

☑ Create or invest in **disruptive technologies and industries**

☑ Expand your **influence—speak, write, mentor, and lead in your field**

☑ Set up **philanthropy or legacy projects** to make a lasting impact

Year 10: Achieve Financial Freedom & Create Generational Wealth

By this stage, you're **financially free**—but wealth isn't just about money. It's about **freedom, legacy, and impact.**

Your action plan:

☑ Ensure your wealth **continues growing through smart investments**

☑ Mentor and build the next generation of leaders and entrepreneurs

☑ Live life on your terms—travel, give back, and enjoy financial freedom

☑ Pass on wealth **the smart way** (trusts, family offices, and legacy planning)

Final Thoughts: The Billionaire Mindset for the Next 10 Years

Wealth isn't built overnight, but if you follow this roadmap with **discipline and strategy**, you'll be in the top 1% within a decade. Stay focused, keep learning, and always think **bigger.** Your 10-year billionaire journey starts today.

11

Purpose-Driven Wealth – Making Money with Meaning

The Billionaire Approach to Legacy and Impact

For the ultra-wealthy, money isn't just about luxury—it's about **leaving a mark on the world.** While many people chase wealth for personal gain, billionaires who build **lasting legacies** focus on something much bigger: **impact.**

The truth is, financial success alone doesn't create fulfilment. The wealthiest and most influential people understand that **true success is measured by what you build, who you help, and the difference you make long after you're gone.**

Step 1: Shift from Success to Significance

At some point, billionaires realize that more money won't change their lives—but **what they do with it will.** They shift from simply accumulating wealth to **creating significance.**

Instead of asking, *"How much can I make?"* they ask:

- *"What problem can I solve?"*

- *"Who can I help?"*

- *"What kind of world do I want to leave behind?"*

This shift is what separates billionaires who **create legacies** from those who are simply rich.

Step 2: Build Something Bigger Than Yourself

Billionaires don't just think about the next **quarter—they think in decades, even centuries.** The wealthiest families and entrepreneurs create **foundations, institutions, and businesses that last generations.**

Take Andrew Carnegie. He didn't just make millions in steel—he used his fortune to build **libraries, universities, and institutions** that still shape the world today. Jeff Bezos isn't just focused on Amazon—he's investing in **space exploration** to redefine the future of humanity.

Your action plan:

☑ **Identify your cause** – What issue in the world matters most to you?

☑ **Create something lasting** – A business, foundation, or fund that continues to grow.

☑ **Think beyond your lifetime** – How will your impact continue for future generations?

Step 3: Use Wealth as a Tool for Change

Money itself isn't the goal—it's the **fuel** for innovation, progress, and transformation. The wealthiest people don't hoard their money—they **deploy it strategically** to drive change.

Here's how billionaires use their wealth for impact:

☑ **Philanthropy with purpose** – Bill Gates funds global health and education through the Gates Foundation.

☑ **Impact investing** – Funding startups that solve real-world problems (like Elon Musk with clean energy).

☑ **Mentorship & knowledge sharing** – Teaching future leaders and entrepreneurs to multiply their impact.

The key is **not just giving money away—but putting it where it will create the most lasting change.**

Step 4: Create Generational Wealth with a Mission

Many billionaires focus on **teaching their children and successors how to manage wealth with purpose.** They don't just pass down money—they pass down **values, knowledge, and a vision for impact.**

Instead of letting their heirs waste their fortune, they ensure their legacy **continues to grow and contribute.**

☑ **Family foundations** – Structuring wealth to fund future philanthropy and innovation.

☑ **Education & mindset training** – Teaching the next generation how to build and sustain impact-driven wealth.

☑ **Long-term planning** – Setting up trusts and investment structures to **preserve and expand wealth responsibly.**

The most powerful legacies aren't just about money—they're about **changing lives, industries, and the world.**

Final Thoughts: Make Your Wealth Matter

At the end of the day, the richest and most respected individuals aren't remembered for how much they had—but for **what they built, who they helped, and the impact they made.**

If you want to create **true, lasting wealth**, ask yourself:

✔ *What do I want to be known for?*

✔ *How can I use my money to make a difference?*

✔ *What legacy will I leave behind?*

Billionaires think beyond themselves. **They create, contribute, and change the world.** And that's what separates them from everyone else.

Wealth Beyond Money: Building a Life That Matters

True wealth isn't just about how much money you have—it's about the **life you build, the people you impact, and the purpose that drives you.** The richest people in the world don't just measure their success by their bank accounts. They focus on something far greater: **a life that matters.**

Think about it—what's the point of having millions (or even billions) if your days feel empty? If your success doesn't inspire you? If your relationships suffer, your health declines, and you feel no sense of purpose? **Real wealth is about creating a fulfilling, meaningful life—not just stacking up numbers.**

Step 1: Redefine What Wealth Means to You

The world teaches us that wealth is about **cars, mansions, and luxury vacations.** But look at the most successful, purpose-driven individuals, and you'll see a different definition.

Wealth is:

☑ **Freedom** – The ability to live life on your terms.

☑ **Impact** – Making a difference in people's lives.

☑ **Time** – The power to spend your days doing what matters most.

☑ **Health** – A strong body and sharp mind to enjoy your success.

☑ **Relationships** – Deep, meaningful connections with the people you love.

The wealthiest, happiest people **design their lives** around these principles. They don't just chase money—they chase **fulfilment.**

Step 2: Align Your Work with Your Purpose

Money without meaning is **empty.** That's why many billionaires, after reaching a certain level of financial success, shift their focus from profit to **purpose.**

Ask yourself:

✔ *What excites me?*

✔ *What problem do I want to solve?*

✔ *How can my work contribute to something bigger than myself?*

Your business, investments, or career should do more than just generate income—they should bring **personal fulfilment and positive impact.** When you align your wealth-building with your **passion and purpose,** money becomes a tool for something greater.

Step 3: Invest in What Truly Matters

The happiest and most successful people understand that **some things are more valuable than money.**

Here's where they invest their time and energy:

☑ **Personal Growth** – Constantly learning, evolving, and improving.

☑ **Health & Well-being** – Exercising, eating well, and prioritizing mental clarity.

☑ **Relationships** – Spending time with family, mentors, and people who inspire them.

☑ **Experiences** – Traveling, learning new skills, and making unforgettable memories.

Because at the end of the day, **the richest person isn't the one with the most money—it's the one with the most meaningful experiences.**

Step 4: Give Back and Create a Legacy

Real wealth isn't just about what you accumulate—it's about what you give. The most successful individuals don't just think about how much they can take; they think about how much they can **contribute.**

The greatest legacies aren't built on **personal gain** but on **helping others.** Whether through philanthropy, mentorship, or innovation, billionaires who leave a lasting impact focus on **making the world better.**

Ways to give back:

✔ **Philanthropy** – Supporting causes you care about.

✔ **Mentorship** – Helping others achieve success.

✔ **Building something that lasts** – Creating businesses, foundations, or initiatives that serve future generations.

Final Thought: True Wealth is a Life Well-Lived

Yes, money can give you choices, comfort, and opportunities. But **real wealth goes beyond money.**

It's about waking up **excited** for your day. Having **the freedom to live life on your terms.** Surrounding yourself with **people who inspire and support you.** Creating something that **outlasts you.**

Success isn't just about making a fortune—it's about **making a difference.** Because at the end of your life, the real question won't be *"How much did I make?"*—it will be *"Did I live a life that truly mattered?"*

The Power of Giving and Philanthropy in True Wealth

The world's wealthiest people understand a simple truth: **real wealth isn't just about what you accumulate—it's about what you give.** Money can buy luxury, but **impact creates legacy.** Philanthropy isn't just an afterthought for the ultra-successful—it's a core part of their wealth-building strategy.

Why the Wealthy Give Back

At a certain point, money alone doesn't bring more happiness. Science backs this up—studies show that after meeting basic needs and financial security, **true fulfilment comes from contributing to something bigger than yourself.**

That's why billionaires like Warren Buffett, Bill Gates, and Oprah Winfrey dedicate massive resources to philanthropy. They understand that **giving isn't just about charity—it's about impact, purpose, and creating lasting change.**

When you give strategically, you don't just help others—you transform yourself.

The Ripple Effect of Generosity

Giving has a multiplying effect. Whether it's **donating money, time, or knowledge,** the impact often extends far beyond what we imagine.

✔ **Education funding** can help one child break the cycle of poverty—leading to generations of success.

✔ **Medical research donations** can lead to breakthroughs that save millions of lives.

✔ **Mentorship and knowledge-sharing** can help the next wave of leaders and innovators rise.

Wealth, when used wisely, has the power to **lift entire communities, drive innovation, and solve global problems.**

Strategic Giving: How the Rich Maximize Impact

The ultra-wealthy don't just give randomly—they give **intentionally.** Here's how they make the most of their philanthropy:

☑ **They align giving with their values.** Instead of spreading donations thinly, they focus on causes they truly care about.

☑ **They use their influence, not just their money.** The wealthy leverage their networks to bring together top minds, governments, and organizations to drive real change.

☑ **They create long-term solutions.** Instead of just donating, they **build systems**—such as foundations, scholarships, and impact-driven businesses—to create **sustainable progress.**

This is why many billionaires **treat giving like an investment.** They look for ways to create the greatest return—not in profits, but in impact.

You Don't Have to Be a Billionaire to Give

Philanthropy isn't just for the super-rich. **Anyone can make a difference.** Whether it's volunteering, mentoring, or donating a small percentage of your income, **giving creates a sense of fulfilment no amount of wealth can buy.**

The key is to start where you are. Ask yourself:

✔ *What causes am I passionate about?*

✔ *How can I give—money, time, or expertise?*

✔ *What small action can I take today to make a difference?*

Even small acts of generosity can **create a ripple effect that changes lives.**

Final Thought: The Legacy of Giving

At the end of life, no one remembers **how much money you had**—they remember **the impact you made.** True wealth isn't just measured by your bank account; it's measured by **the lives you touch.**

Giving isn't just a responsibility—it's a privilege. The greatest reward of wealth isn't in what you keep, but in **what you share with the world.**

Creating a Business That Solves Global Problems

In today's world, businesses aren't just about selling products or services—they're about solving problems. **True wealth** comes when you build a business that addresses the most pressing issues facing our planet, from climate change to inequality to health crises. The most successful entrepreneurs understand that **the key to lasting success** is creating a business that not only profits but **makes a positive impact on the world.**

Why Solving Global Problems is the New Frontier of Business

Global problems aren't just challenges—they are **opportunities**. Every major issue facing humanity today presents a chance for innovative minds to step in and make a difference. And when you solve problems that affect millions or even billions, your business has the power to grow exponentially while **improving lives.**

Billionaires like Elon Musk with **Tesla** and Jeff Bezos with **Amazon** have capitalized on global challenges to build companies that **address climate change, increase efficiency,** and **create new industries**—all while making billions. This isn't by accident; they saw massive global problems and turned them into viable solutions.

How to Build a Business that Solves Global Problems

1. **Identify a Universal Problem**

   Start by identifying a problem that is not just big, but **universal**. Whether it's **clean water, renewable energy, healthcare access,** or **food security,** these are issues that affect people worldwide. The more people you can help, the bigger your potential impact.

2. **Create an Innovative Solution**

Once you've identified the problem, the next step is to think about a **unique solution** that sets your business apart. This isn't about reinventing the wheel—it's about doing things differently, more efficiently, or in a more sustainable way. The **innovation** you bring to the table will drive your business forward, making your solution the **go-to option** for people who need it.

3. **Make It Scalable**

The most successful businesses are those that can scale. If your solution works in one community, can it work in others? If it works in one country, can it be applied globally? Scalability is the key to making a true difference. The more you scale, the more people you can help—and the larger your business becomes.

4. **Build a Business Model with Purpose**

A business with a social purpose is more than just a company—it's a **movement.** When building your business, make sure that your core values and mission are aligned with solving global issues. This will not only attract customers who share those values, but also attract investors who are looking for businesses with **meaning and impact.**

5. **Leverage Technology and Partnerships**

To solve big problems, you need to think beyond the constraints of a traditional business model. **Technology** allows businesses to reach further, scale faster, and implement more effective solutions. **Partnerships** with nonprofits, governments, and other companies can help you expand your impact. The best entrepreneurs **collaborate**, knowing that partnerships are the **fuel** that powers large-scale change.

The Rewards of Purpose-Driven Entrepreneurship

Building a business that solves a global problem isn't just financially rewarding; it's **personally fulfilling**. When you are driven by a cause bigger than profit, you create a sense of purpose that fuels not only your passion but also your resilience.

Moreover, businesses focused on **solving global problems** often attract **loyal customers** who appreciate your commitment to making the world a better place. People today are more likely to support companies that **align with their values**, and as a result, they become your most vocal advocates. **Your business becomes a force for good**, growing through the positive impact it has on people and the planet.

Final Thought: Creating a Legacy of Impact

A business that solves global problems isn't just about generating wealth—it's about **leaving a legacy**. It's about **changing lives, improving communities**, and contributing to the greater good. When you build a company with a **purpose** and a **vision**, you're not just changing your life—you're changing the world.

And that's the kind of wealth that lasts for generations.

12

Become the Billionaire Version of Yourself

The Identity Shift: Seeing Yourself as a Wealth Creator

Becoming the billionaire version of yourself starts with one powerful transformation: shifting your **identity**. It's not just about changing your habits or learning new skills; it's about **changing how you see yourself**. To create wealth, you must first see yourself as a **wealth creator**—someone who is capable of generating abundance, seizing opportunities, and making bold decisions that lead to financial success.

Why Identity Matters in Wealth Creation

Your identity shapes your thoughts, actions, and outcomes. If you view yourself as someone who struggles with money, who always works hard but never gets ahead, or who just isn't "lucky" enough to create wealth, your results will reflect that. But when you see yourself as a **wealth creator**, your mindset shifts. You begin to think and act like someone who attracts wealth, someone who believes that **opportunity** is always within reach.

Billionaires understand this deeply. They don't simply accumulate wealth—they **create it**. They've built their entire mindset around the belief that they have the power to generate wealth from nothing, and that belief is what propels them to take the actions necessary for their success.

How to Shift Your Identity to a Wealth Creator

1. **Change Your Beliefs About Money**

   Most people have limiting beliefs about money: "Money doesn't grow on trees," "I'll never be wealthy," or "I'm not cut out for success." These beliefs hold you back. To become a wealth creator, you need to **rewrite** your money story. Understand that **money is a tool**, and creating wealth is about understanding how to make that tool work for you.

   Billionaires believe that money is abundant, that there is more than enough to go around. This belief shapes how they approach opportunities, investments, and challenges.

2. **See Opportunities, Not Obstacles**

   Shift from focusing on the **obstacles** you face to seeing the **opportunities** that surround you. Instead of thinking, "I don't have enough resources," start thinking, "What resources can I access to make this happen?" Wealth creators are solution-focused. They look at challenges as chances to innovate and **find ways around** the hurdles.

3. **Think Long-Term**

   To be a wealth creator, you must think beyond immediate gratification and **invest in the long game**. Billionaires aren't just focused on making money now—they are focused on creating wealth that **builds over time**. This means investing in yourself, your education, your business, and your relationships. **Patience** and a **long-term vision** are essential in this process.

4. **Develop a Growth Mindset**

   The billionaire mindset revolves around constant growth and learning. If you're not learning, you're falling behind. Wealth creators are always seeking new knowledge, honing their skills, and expanding their **network**. This mindset fuels their ability to adapt and innovate in changing markets, and it's what keeps them ahead of the curve.

5. **Surround Yourself with Wealth Creators**

    Your environment plays a massive role in shaping your identity. If you want to see yourself as a wealth creator, surround yourself with others who think the same way. **Find mentors**, network with successful people, and **engage in communities** that inspire you to think bigger and act bolder. Being around people who share your vision will reinforce your own beliefs about what's possible.

Embody the Wealth Creator Identity

Changing your identity isn't just about thinking differently; it's about **acting differently**. As you see yourself as a wealth creator, your behavior will naturally follow. You'll take calculated risks, make bold moves, and stay committed to your goals. You'll stop letting fear dictate your actions and start making decisions based on your **vision for success**.

Remember, every billionaire started somewhere—often from humble beginnings. What made them successful wasn't just luck or intelligence. It was their unwavering belief in themselves as wealth creators, their refusal to see limitations, and their ability to think and act like someone who **creates wealth on purpose**.

Final Thought: Embrace Your Billionaire Self

The journey to becoming the billionaire version of yourself begins with this one simple but powerful step: **believe you are capable of creating wealth**. The moment you make that shift, you'll begin to attract opportunities, take decisive action, and build a life of financial freedom. Your transformation won't happen overnight, but it will start the moment you decide to see yourself as a wealth creator. **Embrace that identity**, and your wealth will follow.

How to Network with and Learn from Billionaires

If you want to become the billionaire version of yourself, you need to surround yourself with people who have already achieved that level of success. **Networking with billionaires**—and learning from their experiences—can be a game-changer in your journey to wealth. But connecting with people at the top isn't about just shaking hands or exchanging business cards. It's about building **meaningful relationships** that allow you to gain insights, access opportunities, and grow both personally and professionally.

Here's how to network with and learn from billionaires the right way:

1. Shift Your Mindset: Believe You Belong in Their Circle

The first step to networking with billionaires is to **believe you belong** in their circle. Too often, people feel intimidated or unworthy of interacting with high-net-worth individuals. Billionaires are just people—they started with nothing, just like anyone else. The difference is that they **took risks**, **learned from failure**, and never stopped believing in their ability to succeed.

Adopt a mindset of **abundance**. Billionaires are always looking for smart, ambitious, and capable people to collaborate with, and if you show that you have value to offer, they will see you as an equal. Shift from thinking "I'm not worthy" to "What can I contribute?" This change in mindset is key to attracting the right people into your life.

2. Build Your Brand and Reputation

Billionaires are busy. They don't have time to connect with everyone. To get their attention, you need to **build a strong personal brand**—something that sets you apart and makes you valuable. This isn't about boasting, but about showcasing your expertise, passion, and drive.

Focus on what you can offer to others, not just what you can get from them. Whether it's your skills, your knowledge, or your ability to bring people together, find ways to be of service to others in your network. **Offer value before expecting value**. When you do this consistently, you'll create a reputation that attracts the right people—billionaires included.

3. Attend Exclusive Events and Conferences

One of the most effective ways to meet billionaires is by attending **exclusive events**, conferences, and summits where successful entrepreneurs and business leaders gather. Whether it's an industry-specific conference, a charity gala, or an investment summit, these events provide opportunities to connect with people who share your ambition.

But simply attending isn't enough. **Prepare yourself**. Do research on the people who will be there, what they're passionate about, and how your work aligns with theirs. Have a clear value proposition ready—something that intrigues them and shows you're worth their time.

4. Leverage Your Existing Network

If you don't have direct access to billionaires, tap into the network you already have. **Start with people who are one or two steps ahead** of you and ask for introductions to those who are further along the ladder. Wealthy people tend to associate with other wealthy individuals, so gaining access to one influential person can open doors to many more.

Never underestimate the power of a **warm introduction**. People are more likely to respond positively to referrals from trusted contacts. Make sure your network knows who you are and what you're aiming for so they can introduce you to people who can help accelerate your journey.

5. Be Authentic and Value-Driven

When you do get the chance to interact with billionaires, it's crucial to be authentic. **Billionaires value realness**—they can spot someone who's only out for personal gain. Focus on building genuine connections and showing interest in their experiences, rather than just looking for ways to extract value.

Ask questions that show you're genuinely interested in their journey, and don't be afraid to share your own story and vision. The more you show that you're **aligned with their values**—whether it's innovation, wealth-building, or making an impact—the more likely they are to see you as someone they want to spend time with.

6. Learn from Their Success (and Their Failures)

Networking with billionaires isn't just about asking for help; it's about **learning** from their experiences. Billionaires have often encountered significant challenges and failures along the way, but they've learned from those moments and used them as stepping stones to their success. When you have the chance to talk with them, ask about their **lessons learned**, mistakes, and how they overcame obstacles.

You can also **learn through their actions**. Pay attention to the businesses they invest in, the causes they support, and the people they surround themselves with. By observing how they behave and the decisions they make, you can gain priceless insight into what it takes to build wealth on a massive scale.

7. Be Persistent but Patient

Building relationships with billionaires takes time. Don't expect immediate results or quick access to their inner circle. **Persistence is key**. Keep showing up, offering value, and building your reputation. But also be **patient**. These relationships won't happen overnight, and you'll likely face rejection or indifference along the way. But if you continue to stay authentic and focused on your long-term goals, opportunities will begin to open up.

Final Thought: The Power of Proximity

In the world of billionaires, **proximity is power**. The closer you get to these high-level individuals, the more you learn and the more opportunities you create for yourself. By networking with billionaires and learning from their experiences, you'll gain insights and connections that can **catapult you to the next level** of success.

Remember, billionaires didn't get to where they are alone. They **collaborated**, they **learned from others**, and they created opportunities together. You have the same power to do the same—**start building your network today** and learn from the best.

Breaking Free from Self-Doubt and Taking Massive Action

Self-doubt is one of the most powerful forces standing between you and your dreams. It whispers in your ear, telling you that you're not good enough, that others are more talented, or that you're too late to the game. But here's the truth: **self-doubt is the enemy of progress**. It holds you back, keeps you stagnant, and prevents you from reaching your full potential.

To become the billionaire version of yourself, you need to break free from this cycle of doubt. You need to push past the fear and **take massive action**. Here's how you can do it:

1. Recognize Self-Doubt as a Natural Part of Growth

First, understand that **self-doubt is normal**. Every successful person, from billionaires to entrepreneurs, has experienced it. The difference is they don't let it control them. Instead of avoiding self-doubt or pretending it doesn't exist, they **acknowledge it**. When you feel that voice in your head telling you that you're not enough, recognize it as a sign that you're on the edge of something new and challenging.

Growth only happens when you step outside your comfort zone, and that's when self-doubt usually creeps in. **Embrace the discomfort**—it's a signal that you're about to do something important.

2. Reframe Your Mindset: Fear is Just Energy

The key to breaking free from self-doubt is changing the way you view fear. Instead of seeing fear as something to avoid, **reframe it** as a source of energy. Fear and excitement often feel the same in your body—they both cause your heart to race, your palms to sweat, and your mind to race. The only difference is your interpretation of that feeling.

When you start feeling afraid, instead of backing down, tell yourself: **"This is my energy to move forward. This is my opportunity to grow."** Billionaires don't avoid fear—they use it. They know that **on the other side of fear lies growth**, new opportunities, and massive success.

3. Commit to Action, Even When You Don't Feel Ready

Self-doubt often tells you to wait until you're "ready." But the truth is, you will **never feel completely ready**. There's always more to learn, more to do, and more risks to consider. The key is to **take action anyway**.

You don't need to have all the answers. You don't need to wait for the perfect moment. Just start. **Small actions lead to bigger results**, and those small steps will create momentum. The more you act, the more you'll learn, and the less self-doubt will have power over you.

4. Surround Yourself with Supportive People

Another way to break free from self-doubt is by surrounding yourself with people who believe in you. **Your environment shapes your mindset**. If you're constantly surrounded by negative voices or people who don't believe in your dreams, it will be much harder to take action.

Seek out mentors, friends, and like-minded individuals who encourage you to take risks and believe in your potential. **Find people who challenge you** and push you to be better. Their confidence and belief in you will help drown out the voice of doubt in your head.

5. Focus on Progress, Not Perfection

One of the biggest traps that self-doubt sets is the illusion of perfection. It tells you that unless you have everything figured out, you shouldn't take action. But in reality, **perfection is the enemy of progress**.

Instead of waiting for everything to be perfect, focus on making progress. Every step forward, no matter how small, gets you closer to your goal. **Take imperfect action**—billionaires aren't flawless, but they're willing to move forward anyway. Their success comes from taking consistent, courageous action over time, not from waiting for the perfect conditions.

6. Celebrate Small Wins and Build Confidence

As you begin to take action, **celebrate every small win**. Each step forward is proof that you're capable and that you can overcome self-doubt. These small wins build your confidence and keep you motivated.

Remember, success doesn't happen overnight. It's the result of countless small actions, compounded over time. Celebrate your victories, no matter how small they may seem—they're steps in the right direction.

7. Keep Your Eyes on the Bigger Picture

When self-doubt strikes, it's easy to get stuck in the details and lose sight of the bigger picture. Billionaires don't focus on the fear of failure or the obstacles in front of them—they keep their eyes on their ultimate vision. They remember why they started, what their mission is, and what they're working towards.

When self-doubt creeps in, remind yourself of your **why**. Why do you want to succeed? What impact do you want to make? Your purpose will always be a stronger motivator than the temporary discomfort of doubt.

8. Stay Relentless: Never Give Up

The most successful people aren't the ones who never face doubt—they're the ones who **keep going** despite it. They know that every setback is just a setup for a bigger comeback. They understand that success isn't a straight line, but a series of ups and downs.

Billionaires face rejection, failure, and doubt constantly. But they keep going because they **stay relentless**. They don't let temporary setbacks define them. They **take massive action** and keep moving forward no matter what.

Final Thought: Take the Leap

To become the billionaire version of yourself, you must break free from the grip of self-doubt. **You'll never feel 100% ready**—and that's okay. What matters is that you **take massive action**. Each action you take will build your confidence, expand your opportunities, and move you closer to the life you dream of.

Remember: self-doubt is just a signal that you're on the verge of something great. **Use it as fuel** to take action, learn, grow, and ultimately, transform into the billionaire version of yourself.

The Final Step: Living Your Billionaire Blueprint

The journey to becoming the billionaire version of yourself is not a one-time event. It's a transformation that happens over time, a blueprint that you carefully design and then live out every single day. The final step in this journey is about **fully embodying the life you've envisioned**—making the blueprint you've created not just a plan, but your reality.

1. Own Your Vision

Your blueprint begins with a vision—a clear, bold image of where you want to go and who you want to become. But the final step isn't just about having that vision in your mind; it's about **owning it completely**. This means stepping into it with confidence, making decisions based on it, and ensuring every action you take aligns with it.

When you live by your blueprint, you no longer second-guess your goals or wonder if you're on the right track. **Your vision becomes your guide**. Every choice you make, every business deal you pursue, and every relationship you nurture should be an extension of that vision. You have to live it out loud—every day, without exception.

2. Commit to Excellence

Becoming the billionaire version of yourself means consistently **striving for excellence**. This isn't about perfection—it's about continually pushing your limits, learning, and growing. You set the highest standards for yourself and your work, and you never settle for less than your best.

It's important to understand that wealth creation is a mindset that demands **relentless pursuit of better**. Whether it's refining your skills, mastering new tools, or deepening your expertise, you're always focused on becoming the best version of yourself. Your blueprint doesn't include stagnation; it's about growth, evolution, and constant improvement.

3. Take Massive, Consistent Action

The blueprint you've designed won't create wealth on its own. It requires action. And not just any action, but **massive, consistent action**. Success doesn't happen overnight—it's the result of consistent effort, day in and day out, over months and years.

When you live your blueprint, you take **bold and decisive action**. You don't wait for the perfect moment or for all the stars to align. Instead, you act. Every day. Your actions may be big or small, but they're always in alignment with your vision. Each step forward is a step closer to the life you've mapped out.

4. Build a Legacy, Not Just Wealth

Living your billionaire blueprint is about **more than just accumulating wealth**; it's about creating something lasting. Billionaires understand that true success isn't measured by the number in your bank account—it's about the impact you leave behind.

Focus on building **a legacy**—something that will last long after you're gone. This could mean creating a business that revolutionizes an industry, making philanthropic contributions that change lives, or raising a family that carries your values forward. Your blueprint includes your financial goals, but it also encompasses the greater **purpose and meaning** behind your wealth.

5. Master Your Mindset Daily

Becoming the billionaire version of yourself is largely about mindset. Your blueprint isn't just a plan for what you do, it's a plan for how you think. Billionaires cultivate a mindset of abundance, confidence, and possibility.

To live your blueprint, you need to **nourish your mind daily**. Practice gratitude, meditation, and affirmations. Stay grounded in your vision. Surround yourself with people who uplift you and push you to be better. Keep reading, learning, and expanding your mental capacity. Your mindset is the foundation of everything else—it will either support your vision or hold you back. Make sure it's always working in your favor.

6. Embrace the Journey, Not Just the Destination

While you have a clear vision of your billionaire life, the final step is about understanding that **the journey itself is just as important as the destination**. The day-to-day process of building, learning, and evolving is what shapes you into the person you need to be to live your blueprint.

Success isn't a final, fixed point. It's **an ongoing journey of growth**. When you embrace the process, you'll find fulfilment and joy in the work itself, not just the rewards at the end. Stay present, stay focused, and celebrate each victory along the way.

7. Become the Example for Others

The final step in living your billionaire blueprint is **becoming the example for others**. When you live with purpose, take bold actions, and stay aligned with your vision, you inspire others to do the same. Your success becomes a blueprint for those around you—your family, your employees, your community.

Be a mentor. Share your knowledge. Empower others to create their own versions of success. When you make a habit of living out your blueprint, you create a ripple effect that elevates everyone around you. You don't just create wealth for yourself, you become a force for good in the world.

8. Celebrate Your Transformation

Finally, recognize that you've **transformed**. The billionaire version of yourself is no longer a distant dream—it's who you are today. Celebrate your achievements. Honor the growth you've made. But remember: the transformation never ends. Keep evolving, keep striving, and keep pushing yourself to greater heights.

Living your billionaire blueprint is about more than just financial success. It's about **becoming the best version of yourself** and using your wealth and influence to make a difference in the world. Your blueprint is not a fixed plan, but a dynamic journey that evolves with you as you grow, learn, and expand.

In conclusion, living your billionaire blueprint means committing fully to the vision you've created, taking massive action, and constantly evolving. It's about more than wealth—it's about impact, legacy, and becoming the person you were always meant to be. When you live this way, you'll find that true success comes not just in what you achieve, but in who you become.

13

Final Thoughts & Action Plan

The 90-Day Billionaire Mindset Challenge

The journey to becoming a billionaire begins with mastering your mind. This 90-day challenge is designed to help you develop the mindset, habits, and actions that will set you on the path to true wealth. Each day, you'll take small steps that will compound into huge progress. Your thoughts, habits, and actions will align with the mindset of billionaires, and over the next three months, you will transform your life.

Get ready to change the way you think, act, and see the world.

Day 1-10: Setting the Foundation

Day 1: Define Your Billionaire Vision Write down your long-term vision. Where do you see yourself in 10 years? Be specific. What does your ideal life look like—financially, personally, and professionally? This vision will be your North Star.

Day 2-3: Reprogram Your Money Mindset Identify any limiting beliefs you have about money. Write them down and challenge them. Replace negative thoughts with positive affirmations like "I am worthy of wealth" or "Money is a tool for doing good."

Day 4-5: Practice Gratitude Start each day by writing down three things you're grateful for. Gratitude shifts your mindset from scarcity to abundance, which is key for attracting wealth.

Day 6-7: Visualize Success Spend 5 minutes every day visualizing your success. Picture yourself achieving your financial goals. Feel the emotions tied to success, whether it's freedom, security, or impact. Let this feeling fuel your actions.

Day 8-10: Commit to Consistency Success isn't about big bursts of energy. It's about small, consistent actions. Write down 3 daily habits you can commit to for the next 90 days that will move you toward your vision (e.g., reading, networking, saving, etc.).

Day 11-30: Cultivating the Billionaire Work Ethic

Day 11-15: Develop a Growth Mindset Billionaires see challenges as opportunities. This week, embrace something difficult. It could be learning a new skill, tackling a hard project, or solving a complex problem. Reflect on the lessons learned, not just the outcome.

Day 16-17: Set a Financial Goal Set a financial goal for the next 90 days. Be specific. Do you want to increase your income by a certain percentage? Save a specific amount? Invest in something new? Track your progress daily.

Day 18-20: Prioritize Your Time Billionaires value their time above all else. Start tracking how you spend your time. Are you focused on high-value activities or getting distracted? Every hour you spend should align with your vision and long-term goals.

Day 21-25: Create a Daily Routine Billionaires have strict routines. Develop a morning and evening routine that sets you up for success. Include habits like meditation, exercise, journaling, and goal setting.

Day 26-30: Take Massive Action Start making bigger moves toward your financial goals. Whether it's reaching out to potential partners, investing in education, or taking on a new business opportunity, focus on moving forward each day. Don't wait for perfect conditions.

Day 31-60: Expanding Your Horizons

Day 31-35: Learn from the Best Read biographies, listen to podcasts, or watch interviews of successful billionaires. Learn from their journeys. What habits do they have in common? What challenges did they overcome?

Day 36-40: Build Your Network Reach out to at least five people who can help you on your journey. These could be mentors, investors, or people who are in the industry you want to grow in. Networking is a crucial part of building wealth.

Day 41-45: Focus on Personal Growth Attend a course, seminar, or workshop that expands your knowledge. Billionaires invest in their personal growth and learning. The more you know, the better equipped you'll be to handle new opportunities.

Day 46-50: Cultivate Discipline Discipline is key to billionaire success. Identify one area where you're lacking discipline—whether it's health, time management, or finances—and work on it daily until you develop better habits.

Day 51-55: Take Bigger Risks Billionaires take calculated risks. Start stepping outside your comfort zone. It could be investing in a new business, learning a new skill, or trying a new approach to earning money. The goal is to build confidence in taking action even when things are uncertain.

Day 56-60: Focus on Value Creation Billionaires focus on creating value. Look for opportunities where you can solve problems, innovate, or make life better for others. The more value you create, the more wealth will follow.

Day 61-90: Mastering the Billionaire Mindset

Day 61-65: Develop Emotional Resilience Setbacks are inevitable, but how you handle them matters. Practice emotional resilience by learning how to bounce back from disappointments quickly. Every failure is a lesson on your path to success.

Day 66-70: Automate Your Finances Start automating your income, savings, and investments. Whether it's setting up automatic transfers or using apps that help with investing, automation allows you to make your money work for you without constant effort.

Day 71-75: Invest in Your Future Focus on investments that will bring long-term wealth. Learn about stocks, real estate, or other investment vehicles. Start small but steady. The key to building wealth is getting your money to work for you.

Day 76-80: Embrace Long-Term Thinking Billionaires think in decades, not months. Shift your thinking from short-term gains to long-term growth. Ask yourself, "Where do I want to be in 10 years?" and then make decisions based on that vision.

Day 81-85: Make Big, Bold Moves Now that you've laid the foundation, it's time to scale. Make bold, calculated moves that align with your goals. Launch a new business, scale your current venture, or invest heavily in assets that will grow your wealth.

Day 86-90: Reflect and Adjust Reflect on your progress over the past 90 days. What worked? What didn't? Adjust your plan for the next phase of your journey. Remember, the path to becoming a billionaire is a lifelong process, not a destination.

Final Thoughts:

This challenge isn't about perfection; it's about progress. The goal is to shift your mindset, develop habits, and take consistent action toward your billionaire goals. As you complete this 90-day challenge, you'll not only be building wealth but also developing the discipline, resilience, and focus required for long-term success. Keep this momentum going, and you'll be on your way to creating the life you've always dreamed of.

Are you ready to take action? The journey to your billionaire self starts now!

The Daily Wealth-Building Routine

Success doesn't happen overnight, but with a daily routine designed to build wealth, you're setting yourself up for greatness. This daily routine is designed to focus on the key activities that billionaires prioritize to achieve their wealth. Stick to this routine, and you'll start to see results over time.

Morning: Set the Tone for the Day

1. **Wake Up Early (5:00 - 6:00 AM)** Billionaires understand the power of starting the day ahead of everyone else. Waking up early gives you time to focus, plan, and get ahead. Use this time for yourself, before the world gets busy.

2. **Morning Mindset Practice (10-15 minutes)** Spend 10-15 minutes grounding yourself with positive affirmations and visualizations. Picture your goals and success in vivid detail. Think about the kind of billionaire you want to become and visualize achieving it every single day. This will align your mind with abundance and success.

3. **Exercise and Physical Health (30-60 minutes)** Billionaires know that a healthy body fuels a sharp mind. Whether it's running, yoga, strength training, or a brisk walk, make sure to get your blood pumping. Physical health directly impacts mental clarity, energy levels, and productivity.

4. **Healthy Breakfast and Nutrition** A billionaire's diet focuses on nourishment. Choose a balanced meal full of healthy proteins, healthy fats, and vitamins. Avoid sugar and processed foods that can leave you sluggish and unfocused.

5. **Read or Listen to Educational Content (30-60 minutes)** Billionaires prioritize learning every day. Read a book, listen to a podcast, or watch a video on business, finance, or personal growth. Make sure to focus on material that helps you expand your knowledge and skills, especially in areas that will help you grow wealth.

Daytime: Building Wealth Through Focused Action

6. **Plan Your Day (15-20 minutes)** Start by reviewing your to-do list. Prioritize your tasks by focusing on what will make the biggest impact on your wealth-building journey. The key here is to tackle the most important and challenging tasks first, leaving smaller, less critical tasks for later.

7. **High-Value Work Blocks (90-120 minutes per block)** Billionaires focus on high-impact work that moves them toward their goals. Break your workday into two or three focused blocks of time where you'll work on high-value activities. These could be things like strategic planning, investment research, meeting with potential partners, or working on projects that generate income.

8. **Networking and Relationship Building (30-60 minutes)** Build relationships with mentors, peers, and potential partners. Billionaires know the power of relationships in growing wealth. Reach out to someone in your network, attend a virtual event, or connect with someone who can help you grow professionally or financially.

9. **Take Calculated Risks** Every day, take a small calculated risk that will bring you closer to your billionaire goals. This could be in the form of a new business venture, investing in a new opportunity, or learning a new skill. Billionaires thrive on calculated risk-taking.

10. **Wealth-Building Activities** This could include researching investment opportunities, monitoring the stock market, reviewing real estate deals, or working on a side business. Focus your energy on activities that will directly increase your wealth. Always have your financial goals at the forefront of your mind.

Evening: Reflection and Rest for Tomorrow

11. **Evening Review (15-20 minutes)** Take a moment at the end of the day to reflect on your accomplishments. What went well? What can you improve tomorrow? This time helps you assess your progress and fine-tune your strategy.

12. **Self-Improvement and Growth (30-60 minutes)** Spend time working on personal development. Whether it's reading more, working on a skill, or engaging in a personal project, commit to always improving yourself. Billionaires understand that growth is a lifelong journey, not a destination.

13. **Set Goals for Tomorrow (10 minutes)** Before bed, write down your key goals for the next day. This helps you start tomorrow with a clear focus and the right mindset. You'll also wake up knowing exactly where to direct your energy and efforts.

14. **Rest and Recovery (8 hours of sleep)** To be at the top of your game, rest is essential. Billionaires understand that proper sleep is necessary for productivity, health, and mental clarity. Prioritize 7-8 hours of sleep every night to ensure you're performing at your best.

Weekly Focus

- **Monday: Vision & Strategy Day** Start the week by reviewing your long-term vision and the strategies you're using to get there. Are you on track? What adjustments need to be made? Use Monday to set your goals for the week.

- **Tuesday & Wednesday: Action-Oriented Work** These are your power days. Focus intensely on executing your tasks and goals. These days should be dedicated to high-value, income-generating activities.

- **Thursday: Learning & Growth** Dedicate Thursdays to expanding your knowledge and skillset. This is the perfect day for reading, attending seminars, or talking to mentors.

- **Friday: Review & Plan for the Next Week** Reflect on the progress you've made this week. Celebrate the wins, learn from the losses, and make adjustments for the next week. Set yourself up for success by planning ahead.

Monthly Focus

At the start of each month:

- Review your financial goals and assess your progress. Are you hitting your targets? What needs improvement?

- Take time to review your investments and adjust them based on market conditions.

- Evaluate your business ventures and explore new opportunities for growth.

- Make time to expand your network—connect with someone new each month who can add value to your wealth-building journey.

Final Thoughts

This daily routine is designed to guide you on your path to becoming a billionaire. By consistently following this routine, focusing on high-value activities, investing in your personal development, and thinking long-term, you're setting yourself up for massive success. Remember, building wealth is a marathon, not a sprint. Stay disciplined, stay focused, and trust that each small action you take will add up to something extraordinary.

Now, get started! Your path to billionaire status begins today.

Your Personalized Billionaire Roadmap

Becoming a billionaire isn't just about hard work and luck—it's about creating a clear, focused plan and sticking to it over time. This roadmap will help you lay the foundation for building wealth, scaling your income, and achieving long-term financial success. Every billionaire has followed a unique path, but they all share a common journey. Now, it's your turn.

Step 1: Define Your Vision

Before you can start building wealth, you need to know **why** you're doing it. Your vision gives you direction and purpose. What is the life you want to live? What problems do you want to solve? Picture the kind of impact you want to make, not just for yourself, but for the world.

- **Action Step:** Write down your long-term vision. Be as specific as possible. Include the type of business or investment you'll be involved in, the kind of lifestyle you want, and the legacy you want to leave behind.

Step 2: Build the Right Mindset

To become a billionaire, you need the mindset of one. Billionaires think differently—about money, risk, opportunity, and their place in the world. They embrace failure as part of the process, believe in their own abilities, and stay focused on long-term goals.

- **Action Step:** Spend at least 15 minutes each morning on mindset practice. Read affirmations, visualize your goals, and remind yourself of your "why." Train your mind to think like a billionaire.

Step 3: Focus on High-Value Skills

Billionaires don't just work—they work smart. They focus on building high-value skills that will help them make more money, solve bigger problems, and increase their impact. It could be investing, sales, leadership, or anything that brings high returns.

- **Action Step:** Identify the top 2-3 skills you need to master. Break them down into daily learning activities. Commit to constant improvement, whether through reading, taking courses, or seeking mentorship.

Step 4: Create and Scale a Business

Many billionaires reach their wealth through successful businesses. Whether it's a tech company, a product, or a service, you need to create something that meets a large need and scales quickly. The bigger the problem you solve, the more money you can make.

- **Action Step:** Decide what kind of business you want to start or scale. Start by identifying a problem you can solve. Focus on ways to automate, scale, and optimize your business to reach more people and increase profits.

Step 5: Invest Like a Billionaire

Billionaires don't just earn—they invest. They understand the power of compound growth and diversifying their wealth. They invest in stocks, real estate, businesses, and more. It's not about getting rich quickly—it's about making your money work for you.

- **Action Step:** Learn about different investment vehicles (stocks, real estate, startups). Start small and gradually increase your investments as you gain knowledge. Diversify your portfolio to spread risk and increase opportunities for growth.

Step 6: Build Strategic Partnerships

No billionaire achieves success alone. They build strong relationships with mentors, partners, and other successful individuals. Strategic partnerships can help you scale faster, find new opportunities, and access valuable resources.

- **Action Step:** Network regularly with other successful people in your field. Find mentors who can guide you and peers who can help you grow. Look for partnerships that align with your goals and help you reach them faster.

Step 7: Master Wealth Protection

As you build wealth, you must protect it. Billionaires are careful with their money, ensuring it is shielded from taxes, inflation, and risks. They use trusts, offshore accounts, and other strategies to keep their wealth secure.

- **Action Step:** Consult with financial experts to create a wealth protection plan. Learn about tax strategies, asset protection, and legal structures that can help you minimize risks and preserve your wealth.

Step 8: Embrace Risk and Take Action

Billionaires are not afraid to take risks. But they take **calculated risks**—risks that have the potential to pay off big. Every step you take in your journey will require you to step outside your comfort zone. But with every risk comes the potential for massive rewards.

- **Action Step:** Identify a small, manageable risk you can take today. This could be launching a new product, investing in something new, or taking a leap of faith with a business decision. Start small, but keep moving forward.

Step 9: Focus on Continuous Growth

Wealth isn't static—it's dynamic. Billionaires never stop learning and growing. They read books, attend seminars, learn from their failures, and look for new ways to innovate and improve. Growth is a mindset, and it requires constant effort.

- **Action Step:** Dedicate at least one hour every week to learning. Read books, attend events, or seek out new mentors. Always be on the lookout for ways to level up your knowledge and skills.

Step 10: Make a Lasting Impact

Wealth creation is about more than just money—it's about making an impact. Billionaires are driven by a desire to change the world, solve problems, and leave a lasting legacy. Building wealth without a purpose can leave you feeling empty. Having a bigger purpose gives you direction and fulfilment.

- **Action Step:** Identify a cause or problem you care about deeply. What change do you want to see in the world? Begin taking small steps to use your wealth and influence for a greater good.

Final Thoughts

This roadmap is your path to becoming the billionaire version of yourself. It won't be easy, and it won't happen overnight. But with determination, a clear plan, and consistent action, you'll begin to see the results of your efforts.

Remember, billionaires don't just chase money—they chase opportunities, growth, and impact. Follow this roadmap, stay focused, and soon enough, you'll be on your way to living a life beyond your wildest dreams.

Now, take action. Your billionaire journey starts today.

Conclusion

Congratulations! By taking the time to read this book and follow the steps laid out, you've already taken the most important step toward becoming the billionaire version of yourself. But remember, this is just the beginning. The principles, strategies, and insights shared here are tools—tools that will help you build a future of wealth, purpose, and impact.

The path to becoming a billionaire is not easy, but it is clear. It requires vision, mindset, action, and relentless persistence. You've learned how to think like the ultra-wealthy, how to scale your income, and how to protect and grow your wealth. You've discovered the art of strategic investments, deal-making, and building partnerships with the right people. You've even started to build the foundation for a legacy that extends far beyond money.

But let's not forget one of the most important lessons: The journey to wealth is as much about personal transformation as it is about financial success. To become a billionaire, you must first see yourself as one. Shift your mindset, embrace failure as a stepping stone, and always push yourself to learn more, adapt faster, and do better. Your growth will reflect in the opportunities you attract, the decisions you make, and the impact you have on the world.

Now, it's time to **take action**. The blueprint has been laid out for you, and it's in your hands to put it into practice. Each day, take small steps toward your vision. Don't wait for the perfect moment, because the perfect moment doesn't exist. Your actions, no matter how small, will build momentum that leads you closer to your goals.

The road ahead may be challenging. You'll face setbacks, doubts, and obstacles— but that's part of the process. Remember, every successful billionaire has encountered failure, only to rise stronger and wiser. The key is to keep moving forward, stay focused, and trust in the process.

You are capable of building wealth not just for yourself, but for those around you. You have the power to create a life that reflects your deepest values, to solve problems that impact millions, and to leave a legacy that outlasts you. This journey is about **making money with meaning**, and your wealth will be the tool to make a real difference in the world.

As you step forward, hold on to this truth: Becoming a billionaire isn't just about reaching a financial goal; it's about living a life of purpose, growth, and continuous improvement. And when you look back on your journey, you'll see that the true value wasn't just in the wealth you created—but in the person you became along the way.

Now, go out and build the life you've always dreamed of. The world is waiting for your greatness. Your billionaire journey starts now.

References

Although this book is original work and references are not relevant, I have provided a few other books that discuss financial concepts if you wish to extend your reading in this area.

☐ Carnegie, A. (2006). *The Art of Money Getting: Golden Rules for Making Money.* Cosimo, Inc.

☐ Kiyosaki, R. T. (2017). *Rich Dad Poor Dad: What the Rich Teach Their Kids About Money That the Poor and Middle Class Do Not!* Plata Publishing.

☐ Robbins, T. (2020). *Money: Master the Game – 7 Simple Steps to Financial Freedom.* Simon & Schuster.

☐ Sharma, R. (2021). *The 5 AM Club: Own Your Morning. Elevate Your Life.* HarperCollins Publishers.

☐ Sweeney, T. (2022). *Billionaire Mindset: The Key Principles of Ultra-Wealthy Entrepreneurs.* Wealth Publishing.

☐ Thiel, P. (2014). *Zero to One: Notes on Startups, or How to Build the Future.* Crown Business.

www.ingramcontent.com/pod-product-compliance
Lightning Source LLC
Chambersburg PA
CBHW030509210326
41597CB00013B/838